ENGLISH ELECTRIC LIGHTNING

XA847

ENGLISH ELECTRIC LIGHTNING

THE RAF'S FIRST MACH 2 FIGHTER

PHILIP BIRTLES

FONTHILL

First published in Great Britain in 2026 by
Fonthill
An imprint of
Pen & Sword Books Ltd
Yorkshire – Philadelphia

ISBN 978-1-03615-684-8

A CIP catalogue record for this book
is available from the British Library.

Typeset in SabonLTStd 10/13 by
SJmagic DESIGN SERVICES, India.
Printed and bound in the UK by CPI Group (UK) Ltd, Croydon, CR0 4YY

MIX
Paper | Supporting
responsible forestry
FSC www.fsc.org FSC® C013604

The Publisher's authorised representative in the EU for product
safety is Authorised Rep Compliance Ltd., Ground Floor,
71 Lower Baggot Street, Dublin D02 P593, Ireland.
www.arccompliance.com

For a complete list of Pen & Sword titles please contact
PEN & SWORD BOOKS LIMITED
George House, Units 12 & 13, Beevor Street, Off Pontefract Road,
Barnsley, South Yorkshire, S71 1HN, England
E-mail: enquiries@pen-and-sword.co.uk
Website: www.pen-and-sword.co.uk

or

PEN AND SWORD BOOKS
1950 Lawrence Rd, Havertown, PA 19083, USA
E-mail: uspen-and-sword@casematepublishers.com
Website: www.penandswordbooks.com

Contents

Introduction

The English Electric Lightning was the first and only RAF fighter aircraft to fly at speeds in excess of Mach 2 and was an effective Cold War deterrent against hostile reconnaissance aircraft from the Soviet Union. It just survived the infamous 1957 Defence White Paper decreeing that all of Britain's future air defence would be by guided missiles, none of which had been developed. What began as a basic high-speed research project grew into a highly capable air defence platform. Its main shortcoming was lack of endurance, but this was usually overcome by frequent in-flight refuelling. It was a challenging aircraft to operate, but once familiar, it was popular with pilots. The Lightning was somewhat daunting for the inexperienced pilot, but once they had mastered thinking ahead to where the aircraft was going to be, many pilots found it a very rewarding and effective fighter. It was also a challenge to maintain, but when established, the ground crews were able to keep the aircraft operational. What started out as the experimental P1, became Britain's last home-produced fighter and was the first RAF fully integrated weapon system.

1
Project Design

The Preston, Lancashire-based English Electric Company (EECo) had produced a series of flying boats in the First World War, but during the Second World War had concentrated on building Hampdens and Halifaxes for the RAF, gaining a reputation for high quality and low cost. After the war, the company then built de Havilland Vampires until 1952 for the RAF, adapting to wooden semi-monocque structure for the pilot pods.

With the company's decision in April 1945 to participate in post-war aircraft manufacture, a design team was formed, headed by W. E. W. 'Teddy' Petter as chief engineer. Petter, who had been responsible for the wartime Westland fighter development, attended a meeting with the RAF Director of Operational Requirements and his staff on 16 June 1948. The following day, he wrote a report which mainly concerned the Canberra jet bomber, but at the end, included a reference to a 'High Speed Fighter'. Although very much a research project at the time, there was the possibility of two or three prototypes and maybe production orders for a supersonic aircraft to sustain the workforce at the Preston factories.

The English Electric design team was created in 1945 to design a jet-powered successor to the Mosquito, which became the Canberra, and Petter's deputy was F. W. 'Freddie' Page. Canberra design followed by what was to become the P1 and later, the Lightning. Initial proposals were created from research by the RAE Farnborough, but there was also access to a vast amount of information captured from Germany at the end of the war.

One of the major challenges was to overcome the barrier of compressibility where drag reached a level when the aircraft would go no faster. At above 90 per cent of the speed of sound, there appeared to be insurmountable problems of instability and controllability, which had already been experienced, but German research had also looked into sweptback wings which appeared to show some promise. It was believed that wing leading edge sweep back could help in smoothing compressibility shock waves. With the Canberra jet bomber capable of reaching 50,000 feet, the team realised none of the current RAF jet fighters could intercept it, making an answer to compressibility problems a priority.

The Preston-based EECo design team were working on the concept of a supersonic fighter and the challenge of compressibility needed to be overcome. Trials with a Meteor IV flying from Warton only confirmed the urgent need for a fighter with a high-level flight supersonic performance. Reports were also coming in from America of successful supersonic flights with the Bell X-1 and North American XP-86 Sabre, creating considerable interest from government departments, particularly the latter with swept wings and tailplane, which had obviously overcome major compressibility problems. The Sabre prototype was flown by Roland Beamont in June 1948, the results of which gave Petter increased confidence in the proposals.

In the first week of July 1948, Petter received notification from the Ministry of Supply (MoS) giving advanced notification of the issue for a requirement for the design of a transonic aircraft capable of speeds from Mach 1 to Mach 1.4. Although it may not be suitable for operational use, Petter intended to make provision for some of the required operational features. By the end of July, a specification for a transonic aircraft had been issued defining a performance of 700kt at 45,000 feet (M.1.21), increasing to Mach 1.4 with reheat. At full throttle, endurance was to be 10 minutes, plus 15 minutes at economic cruise once operational height had been reached. It was a single pilot crew with option for emergency ejection. The engine configuration included single R-R Avon, multiple Avons with and without reheat, or single jet with rocket boost. A RAE Farnborough report suggested highly swept back wings and a tailplane on top of the fin.

As early as 16 July 1948, the first schemes had been drawn by the English Electric design team at Warton, with a contract received on 3 August. Four further layouts were produced by the end of July, two with a pair of Avons and another two with a pair of what was to become Armstrong Siddeley Sapphires. The engines were mounted one above the other to minimise frontal area and reducing drag. Further, more radical studies included a butterfly tail and annular air intake. German research covered the benefits of swept wings and reduced thickness, but it was essential to gain first-hand experience specific to their design challenges. This resulted in a large investment in test facilities, including wind tunnels which were initially used for Canberra development. By October the butterfly tail had small fins at the tips with the upper engine in the forward position. Both unarmed and armed versions were offered and power was to be from two 7,500lb thrust Sapphire engines. A brochure was submitted to MoS on 3 November. By the end of the year a contract had been placed for two flying prototypes and a structural test specimen to specification F.23/49 for a supersonic research aircraft with fighter development potential.

Meanwhile, the EECo engineers continued to develop the transonic fighter design, improving the wings and tail, and beginning to consider a single fin. In January 1949 the project was designated P1 by the company, and the following month the single fin was confirmed. There was a RAE conflicting view for swept wing aircraft, that the tailplane should be either on the top, or high up the fin. This configuration was not favoured by the EECo designers, who felt an all-moving tailplane as far below the wing as possible would be most effective. This would be the key to stability for a highly swept wing, providing effective pitch control at all speeds from stall to beyond the speed of sound. This layout completely eliminated pitch problems leading to loss of control in a super stall. The swept wings were, in effect, a delta layout with the inner trailing edges removed and effective control was achieved by mounting ailerons on the wing trailing edges, which were perpendicular to the line of flight. It was also decided to use power controls to provide good lateral control features, which were experienced with the SB.5 manual controls. The primary power controls for the Lightning were the first to be developed in Britain. The decision to adopt a low tail was a result of comprehensive wind tunnel testing at Warton, which was used widely with later fast jet designs into the 1980s.

Although the Sapphire had been chosen for the prototype, power options were still being considered including the R-R Avon and the possibility of reheat. By mid 1949, the installation of RA.4 Avons was being explored with design discussions with Rolls-Royce (R-R) on intake and jet pipe design. The possibilities of a single large engine were investigated, but no single engine existed with the power required. A single engine would also create weight and balance problems, and even a group of three jet engines were considered and rejected. Finally, on 20 March 1950, the MoS made a firm commitment of Sapphires for the prototypes.

By 30 December 1949, the RAF were circulating a draft operational requirement for an operational transonic fighter, and on 23 March 1950 it was decided to award a contract to Specification F.23/49 to English Electric to fulfil Operational Requirement OR.268. A pure simple single engine research aircraft to E.16/49 was to be developed more quickly and cheaply, which resulted in the Fairey FD.2 being ordered on 26 September 1950.

The boffins at Royal Aircraft Factory (RAE) Farnborough had some doubts about EECo P1 highly swept wing design at low speeds. On 25 October 1950, the MoS were persuaded to issue Specification ER.100 to produce an aircraft to compare low speed characteristics between medium and highly swept wings. This resulted in the Short SB.5, although it was unlikely to fly much sooner than the P1, which was scheduled for October 1952. The SB.5 might have been of some use in curing any problems associated with early flight testing of the P1. Both the P1and FD.2 were considered to be Mach 1.5 aircraft by the RAE and MoS, with the step to Mach 2 research aircraft to follow in 1953 to Specification ER134T.

The major aerodynamic challenge was to prove the effectiveness of highly swept wings; the SB.5 helping with low-speed controllability, although the low set tailplane was still not approved by the RAE. Power controls were expected to overcome the low-speed handling problems experienced with the SB.5 manual controls, and a simple solution was a chord-wise slot cut in the wing leading edge instead of wing fences. This was incorporated in the P1 prototype before the first flight and was a complete success.

Despite the MoS considering the P1 as a pure research aircraft with only space provision for operational systems, EECo continued to fulfil the requirements of F.23/49 for a supersonic fighter. Wings and tailplane were to be mounted low on the fuselage. Power was to come from a pair of 8,450lb thrust R-R Avons. Armament was to be two 30mm cannons mounted either side of the cockpit and a radar ranging dish was mounted under an intake lip. However, wind tunnel testing resulted in the wings being moved to halfway up the fuselage and the fore and aft engine positions was reversed. The RAE were still unhappy with the low set tailplane; the SB.5 was also used to investigate different tailplane positions. The name Lightning was adopted in October 1958.

Short SB5 WG768 with 60-degree wing sweep and high mounted tailplane was first flown on 2 December 1952. It is now preserved in the Ulster Museum of Flight ast Long Kesh. (*C. R. Brown*)

The perceived threat at the start of the Cold War in 1949 was from high-flying Soviet strategic bombers potentially armed with nuclear weapons; the threat rapidly evolving, making defending against it very difficult to assess. As a result, the Lightning was not the only project to be plagued by constant revision to requirement. However, with the Lightning being the only survivor of the 1957 Defence White Paper, albeit as an interim, all the other projects competing for funds were cancelled. Lessons learned from problems with earlier projects included ordering development batches for testing and the many trials required, having weapons system teams in the MoS and RAF pilots involved from the early stages of testing.

Petter resigned and was replaced by Freddie Page in February 1950. The challenges of producing an integrated weapons system were increasing costs, and risk, as the systems were not produced by EECo, but developed by other specialist companies working with the prime contractor. Costs rose almost without control due to many changes to the systems specifications and manufacturing was more expensive due to allowing for the higher speed aerodynamic loads on the airframe. Although the P1s would be powered by Sapphire engines, Avon engines were still being considered for developed versions, requiring a dedicated intake and airflow ducting for efficient performance.

Another major consideration was the provision of armament, which for the first time tended towards guided missiles. One of the most promising was the use of infrared homing seeker; initially homing autonomously on the heat of a jet pipe, which was developed by the de Havilland Propeller Company as the Firestreak. The limitation of this missile, was that it was a tail chase attack, which with incoming strategic bombers, was unlikely to be the situation as they would be approaching Britain. If the interceptors were behind, it would be too late. The Firestreak was chosen for the Lightning in 1954 and an all-aspect version which detected surface heat of a hostile airframe was also developed by de Havilland and known as Red Top. This entered service on the Lightning and Sea Vixen in 1964. The other major system development was an air interception (AI) radar, although priority was development of the all-weather larger radars for both the Sea Vixen and Javelin. A day fighter radar ranging was requested by Freddie Page on 7 April 1953 and in December Ferranti proposed a design, followed by the issue of operational requirement OR3572 in July 1954.

Other challenges included development of power controls, auto pilot, ejection seats, navigation and communications equipment, all complicating the overall design progress. However, the Lightning became the first RAF integrated weapon system. Meanwhile EECo continued with overall aerodynamic design to be followed by engine integration.

The Short SB.5 was unlikely to fly much before the P1, but it could be useful to investigate any low-speed problems which might arise. The official specification for the SB.5 was issued on 28 November 1950 with an initial configuration of 50 degrees wing sweep back, full span leading edge flaps and a high mounted tailplane. With the second configuration, the wing sweep was increased to 60 degrees, which the RAE believed would represent any problems anticipated. The third layout was the 60-degree sweep back, small inboard leading-edge flaps and low-set tailplane. The final configuration was to increase wings sweep back to 70 degrees with a return to high-mounted tailplane.

The contract for the first two P1 prototypes was awarded on 1 April 1950, although it was confirmed only space provision for operational equipment which included simple radar ranging and cannon armament. By July 1951, there were concerns within the British aerospace industry regarding the growing weight and costs of the uncontrolled additional systems and equipment to be incorporated in the aircraft. An earlier example was the Hawker Hunter, which had experienced a dramatic rise in weight and consequent loss in performance caused by the addition of various items of equipment to the basic design. This resulted in the difficult choice between performance, systems and cost. As a result, it was agreed that airframe designers be consulted at earlier stages of defining the requirement and specification.

With the detailed design of the first prototype progressing, at a meeting on 9 January 1952, it was agreed more prototypes would be needed and as a result three more aircraft were to be ordered armed with four 30mm cannons. EECo submitted its detailed specification for the third and subsequent prototypes on 18 June 1952, with the designation P1B, the first two prototypes then becoming P1As. The major difference was the nose section from the transport joint just aft of the cockpit, which began to look like the Lightning.

The new intake allowed an increase in speed from 1.56 to 1.68 and the conical centre nose section provided room for a ranging radar. The new canopy improved all-round view for the pilot. In June 1952, a Blue Jay, later to become Firestreak, armament was illustrated, together with a 300-gallon under-fuselage ventral tank to extend endurance.

Meanwhile, the SB.5 was first flown on 2 December 1952 with the 50-degree wing, but would not fly in the P1A configuration until January 1954, when the P1A was nearly complete. It did, however, demonstrate correctly the EECo wind tunnel data, as far as handling characterises were concerned; its most useful purpose was to allow Roland Beamont, the chief test pilot, to familiarise himself with the handling of a highly swept wing. With the P1A powered by two 7,200lb thrust un-reheated Sapphire engines, it was expected to exceed Mach 1 in level flight. The designed landing speed was to be 160kt, with contingency plans to cope with 180 or 200kt, with wheels, tyres and brakes designed to be capable of 220kt landings.

The original intention was to power the P1Bs with Sapphire engines, but due to range difficulties, the R-R RA24 Avon overcame the endurance limitations and gave a significant increase in overall performance without major structural modifications. It was expected to reach up to 60,000-foot ceiling and achieve Mach 2. In addition to the five prototypes, a total of twenty pre-production aircraft were planned to cover the wide range of operational and development testing required. The development batch would be built using limited jigs and tools, making way for the later full production programme.

The prototype P1A WG760 was first flown by Roland Beamont from Boscombe Down on 4 August 1954 and exceeded Mach 1 on 11 August without the benefit of reheat. Despite the predictions by the RAE, the aircraft was free of any major aerodynamic or structural problems.

Roland Beamont lifts the P1A prototype off the Boscombe Down runway for its first flight on 4 August 1954. (*BAE Systems*)

Design work now concentrated on the weapons system development, covering radar, armament and cockpit displays for single-seat, all-weather operations. Ferranti were continuing to design the AI 23 which was intended for the Lightning specific needs. The competing Radar Research Establishment (RRE) was attempting to design a radar capable of being used widely over a number of projects, which would be a compromise for all users.

The main armament for the Lightning was to be air-to-air missiles, with guidance options including beam riding, command guidance and semi-active homing, but all these options presented problems. Design then proceeded on Blue Jay during 1955 and 1956 to assess its effect on aircraft performance, proceed with detail design of the installation and develop the missile aiming and firing options. Additional development work was being undertaken by de Havilland Propellers on achieving a higher altitude performance with larger wings and a more sensitive seeker head. Blue Jay Mk.1, which was adopted as Firestreak for the Lightning as a tail chase infrared weapon with hot jet pipes as the target heat source.

After making fifty test contractor flights the first P1A was handed over to the A&AEE at Boscombe Down on 9 March 1955. It was joined in the test programme by the second prototype WG763 on 18 July 1955 and as well as continuing on performance and handling development, was also fitted with a pair of 30mm cannons mounted in either side of the upper nose for weapons trials from January 1956. Draft Specification F.23/49 was issued on 24 February 1956 defining the build standard of the three P1Bs and 20 development batch, but it was not published for a year to clarify some development problems, largely due to inconsistencies with the integrated weapons system policy. Too many of the systems to be added were out of control of the aircraft manufacturer. This resulted in English Electric being responsible for the total integration of the aircraft and its equipment.

By the end of 1955, testing of Blue Jay showed good results, giving EECo confidence for testing on the P1B, allowing detailed design to proceed. Infrared homing missiles

P1A second prototype WG763 at Warton being prepared for its first flight, on 18 July 1955 by Roland Beamont. (*BAE Systems*)

were smaller and lighter than radar-guided missiles. Before A&AEE weapons testing, Blue Jay had to be cleared on the P1 with one prototype and four development aircraft allocated to missile development trials. EECo, de Havilland Propellers and Ferranti continued to work together, studying Blue Jay Mk.3, an all-aspects missile, which later became Red Top. Both IR and radar guidance were being considered, although the IR version was favoured for the Lightning due to its cloud-free, high-altitude target threats.

From July 1954, a new Defence Policy issued by the Chiefs of Staff responded to the increasing threat of ballistic missiles and nuclear weapons. The government was also urging for reductions in the defence budget, questioning the value and effectiveness of many of the current programmes, leading to a series of cuts and cancellations. A development of the Swift, Type 545 and the Thin Wing Javelin were both cancelled by June 1956. From February 1957, a number of other projects came into focus, and the Air Council agreed to the cancellation of the Fairey Delta fighter development and the mixed power-plant SR.177. Britain's main air defence would concentrate on the development of surface-to-air guided weapons (SAGW), including an anti-missile capability. These cancellations were then announced by Duncan Sandys in the April 1957 Defence White Paper.

Meanwhile F.23/49 was still going ahead, armed with a pair of Blue Jays and to be equipped with AI.23 radar. On 4 April 1957, the first P1B XA847 was flown and exceeded the speed of sound during this flight. Blue Jay test firings had scored eight hits out of fifteen firings and out of twenty acceptance trial firings there had been thirteen hits.

Lightning development was therefore able to proceed using the development batch to define the initial production versions, leading to the service entry of the more effective F.Mk.3, responsible for the air defence of Britain. Later, it served in the NATO front line in Germany as well as Cyprus and Singapore in its ultimate versions until its retirement in 1988. English Electric was pioneering in the development of the all-new concept of a Mach 2 fighter.

P1B first prototype XA847 taxiing and was first flown from Warton by Roland Beamont on 4 April 1957. This was the first to be powered by R-R Avon engines. (*BAE Systems*)

2

Flight Testing

The P1 prototype WG760 was moved to Boscombe Down by road in June 1954, where it was reassembled ready for final systems checks prior to engine runs. These started in July, followed by taxi runs from 24 July with 125kt achieved on the first day, allowing the nose wheel to lift. As confidence increased, short hops were started on 26 July which demonstrated the P1 was stable and responsive in all axes for take-off and landing. The tests could easily be accommodated on Boscombe's 3,000-yard runway without overheating the brakes. On 4 August, the weather was slightly misty, mostly with thin high cloud, and visibility improved by 10.00 hrs, allowing the first flight to be scheduled for 11.00 hrs. Roland Beamont climbed into the cockpit and Peter Hillwood taxied out in a Canberra as the 'chase' aircraft. Beamont taxied to the 24 runway threshold and commenced the take-off. With the nose wheel lifted at 120kt, the aircraft became easily airborne at approximately 145kt and started its climb with the undercarriage retracted at around 160kt, and power reduced to maintain a shallow climb at 200kt. Flaps were retracted at 210kt and aircraft trim throughout was maintained. Altitude was increased to 8,000–9,000 feet where Indicated Air Speed (IAS) was gradually increased to 400kt with no buffeting or roughness. Height was increased to between 13,000 and 14,000 feet with IAS up to M 0.75, with control effectiveness and systems being checked continually. With the fuel levels declining, the Boscombe circuit was rejoined and undercarriage selected down, followed by the flaps. Touchdown was made at 140kt and braking was assisted by the deployment of a tail-mounted break chute.

The aircraft was checked overnight and was found to be fully serviceable ready to begin the process of attaining level supersonic flight. The prototype was flown the next day on control and trim change checks.

With growing confidence in the aircraft, the P1 was levelled over the Solent in clear weather and turned up the Channel on 11 August. Speed was gradually increased to M 0.9 with no sign of compressibility or buffet. All was clear for selection of full power which was increased to 100 per cent. The Mach meter increased to 0.95 with good stability increasing to Mach 0.98 where acceleration appeared to stop and despite maintaining full power at 30,000 feet, the speed failed to further increase. With the distance from Boscombe rapidly increasing, power was reduced and a return made to base. On analysis of the performance results, it was found that Mach 1 true had been achieved, and a further half minute of acceleration would have confirmed Mach 1 on the instruments.

Above: P1A prototype WG760 in final assembly at Warton. (*BAE Systems*)

Below: P1A prototype WG760 original publicity photo at Boscombe Down, not giving much away in terms of wing planform. (*BAE Systems*)

Above: P1A prototype WG760 being pushed out of the hangar at Boscombe Down in preparation for running the Sapphire engines. (*BAE Systems*)

Below: P1A WG760 ready for engine runs at Boscombe Down in preparation for first flight. (*BAE Systems*)

Above: Prototype P1A WG760 taxi trials on the Boscombe Down runway, ready for first flight. (*BAE Systems*)

Below: The first P1A WG760 touches down on the Boscombe Down runway after a successful first flight. (*BAE Systems*)

Following a detailed engineering check to correct the earlier snags—ready for a busy test programme, the fourth flight was made on 13 August. Mach 1.01 was recorded and continued to gradually increase to Mach 1.08 allowing control checks to be made. As a celebration on the approach towards Boscombe, Beamont put the aircraft into a gentle dive at 35,000 feet, increased power to Mach 1.02, planting a sonic bang on the airfield.

With a transonic capability confirmed, flight testing continued to check basic stability and control up to Mach 1.14. The priority was to return the prototype to Warton, but the runway extension had only reached 2,000 yards and the next priority was to check landing performance, when a long runway would be essential. With a high level of serviceability, the aircraft was performing well, making three flights on 26 August and four on 15 September—the only delays caused by occasional poor weather. Despite the good level of flying, only 8.5 hours had been achieved by the Farnborough Air Show start, not meeting the minimum of 10 hours for a new type. After the Farnborough show, the remaining tests were completed with handling problems cured and basic engineering systems found reliable.

Finally, the prototype was flown to Warton on 23 September in a time of just over 17 minutes with Warton in sight, the 200 miles flown at 32,000 feet, allowing a highly successful flight test programme to continue, bringing total flights to fifty in 33.53 hours. Mach limitations were increased to 1.2 with Mach 1 exceeded forty times.

Back at Warton, WG760 proved its reliability, allowing the expansion of the transonic flight envelope, proving its handling and performance in preparation for the more representative P1B, with minimum delays due to weather in the winter of 1954/55. Following the A&AEE assessments, Des de Villiers joined the P1A test

P1A WG760 making an overshoot after returning to Warton following initial flight trials at Boscombe Down. (*BAE Systems*)

Above: P1A WG760 public debut flown by Roland Beamont at the Farnborough Air Show in September 1954. (*BAE Systems*)

Below: P1A prototype WG760 late in its flight development programme testing the cambered wing leading edge shape. (*BAE Systems*)

flying team in December 1954, followed by Peter Hillwood early in 1955. The 100th Mach 1 test flight was achieved in the spring of 1955, demonstrating its role as a high-performance fighter. By this stage, it was possible to investigate the acquisition of targets in excess of Mach 1, which was achieved successfully. A major problem was the loss of the canopy at high speed three times, resulting in re-engineering the canopy locking system, which eliminated the difficulty.

The next stage in the flight development programme was to increase the speed to Mach 1.5 and change to reheat Sapphires with 9,200lb thrust. This meant that WG760 was grounded for modifications in October 1955. It flew again on 31 January 1956, by which time the second prototype WG763 had joined the flight development programme on 18 July 1955. Meanwhile, with the more powerful engines, climb to 40,000 feet was achieved in a mere 3.5 minutes and level performance was increased incrementally from M 1.4. As a result of these tests M 1.53 was reached, but could not go beyond due to inadequate fin area, which provided data for the P1B fin redesign. The reheat system proved unsatisfactory and flying resumed in early June with cold thrust engines.

The P1A had inadequate endurance, and to help improve the range, WG763 was fitted with a ventral fuel tank, taking total fuel capacity from 5,000lb to 7,000lb, increasing flight time from an average of 30 minutes with the reheat prototype to 45 minutes to one hour, this aircraft was allocated to gun trials.

With the completion of the initial flight development programme covering performance, stability and control, the first prototype was grounded for major

Both P1A prototypes outside the flight test hangar at Warton being prepared for the day's flight development programme. (*BAE Systems*)

Above: P1A WG760/7755M by RAF Henlow parade ground on 27 March 1967 in AFDS markings. This aircraft was first flown by R. P. Beamont on 4 August 1954 and allocated to development flying with final grounding on 7 June 1962 after 268 hours 17 minutes flying. It was allocated to Warton as an instructional airframe in August 1982, moving to St Athan in September 1965. It was moved to Henlow in November 1966 and put in the care of RAF Binbrook on 29 July 1982 for preservation. It was allocated to RAF Museum Cosford on 6 May 1985 and delivered in January 1986. (*Philip Birtles*)

Below: P1A WG763 at RAF Henlow in October 1964. This aircraft was first flown on 18 July 1955 and after its flight development programme, was grounded on 5 August 1963 and moved to Henlow. It went to the RAF Museum at Hendon briefly, but was then allocated to the Manchester Museum of Science and Technology, where it arrived on 17 August 1982. It is now with the Boscombe Down Aviation Collection at Old Sarum. (*Philip Birtles*)

modifications. The basic plain 60-degree wing was given increased area by decreasing the sweepback to 55 degrees on the leading edge outboard of the slot. The new leading edge was cambered and it was expected to improve the M 0.9 cruise performance by 15–20 per cent and giving handling benefits. With modifications complete, it was flown again on 15 February 1957, and handling was improved. This modification was not incorporated until much later in Lightning development.

With the Lightning aerodynamic and handling thoroughly investigated, the first P1B XA847 was close to completion. It was similar in aerodynamics, but with new R-R Avon engines and provision for operational systems, development could start on Britain's first day and night, all-weather supersonic interceptor, due for RAF service entry by 1959. Power was from two 11,250lb thrust Avons plus reheat, which increased dry available thrust by more than 50 per cent and the pilot was in a more raised position in the redesigned nose. The new circular air intake housed the Ferranti AI 23 fire control radar and fixed armament was two 30mm Aden guns in the nose. Additional armament could be two more Aden guns in an under-fuselage pack, two de Havilland Firestreaks or forty-eight 2-inch air-to-air unguided rockets. The Lightning could attain over 55,000 feet by a zoom climb. Between 28,000 and 55,000 feet over M 1.7 could be reached, with an expected M 2+ at 36,000 feet. Provision of reaching 60,000 feet was achieved with a jettisonable twin Scorpion rocket pack, providing a further 2,250lb thrust to reach the highest-flying hostile bomber. Fortunately, when Gary Powers was shot down by a Soviet missile at high altitude on 1 May 1960, the need for high-altitude strategic bomber attacks receded; all future threats would come from low level, below radar detection.

The first P1B XA847 was ready to fly on 4 August 1957 and although similar to the P1A, it could still have some challenges, although it was thought unlikely. The test pilot was well-prepared with his knowledge of design characteristics and had worked with the design team for many years. There would also be the benefit of design simulators to predict handling responses. With the aircraft at the end of Warton's runway, power was increased at 12.45 hrs and a climb was made away at 230kt with undercarriage retraction. During the flight, a transition was made through Mach 1 without buffet or vibration, after which a return was made to Warton. The reliability was so high, 100 flights were made by November with speeds in excess of 1,000 miles achieved daily, and M 1.75 (1,161mph) was soon reached with adequate margin to go further. The aircraft was then prepared for the Boscombe Down service evaluation.

Routine test flying continued from Warton to establish the build standard for the pre-production batch Lightning F.1s. With greater utilisation, reheat fire warnings were experienced and it took some two years to resolve, restricting any use of reheat above 20,000 feet. Another major problem was malfunctions of the elaborate warning systems, particularly as it was being pioneered with the Lightning. The reliability of the warning systems was not up to the same high level as the aircraft control systems and engines, and false fire warnings were caused. It took a number of years and many hours flying to bring the warning system to an acceptable service standard, one of the main problems was the wiring. Finally, on 8 May 1958, Jimmy Dell made a precautionary return to Warton with a fire warning illuminated and during the landing roll, the elevators locked solid. He stopped on the runway and when preparing to get out, noticed smoke coming from the rear fuselage. The fire crew found a hole in the aircraft fuselage side with an intense fire burning.

Above: P1B XA847 was demonstrated by Roland Beamont at the Farnborough Air Show in September 1957. (*BAE Systems*)

Below: P1B XA847 over the River Ribble estuary on an early test flight with the fuselage air brakes out. (*BAE Systems*)

Above: P1B XA847 official naming ceremony. (*BAE Systems*)

Below: P1B XA847 with name on the nose. (*BAE Systems*)

Above: P1B XA847 head-on carrying a pair of Firestreak aerodynamic rounds. (*BAE Systems*)

Below: P1B XA847 with dark front fuselage. (*BAE Systems*)

Above: P1B XA847 carrying Red Top aerodynamic rounds and fitted with a dorsal fillet to balance the side loads of the missiles. (*BAE Systems*)

Below: P1B XA847 gravel arrester trials at Farnborough. (*BAE Systems*)

Above: Second prototype P1B XA853 heading a line of development aircraft at Warton with a selection of basic and taller fins. (*BAE Systems*)

Below: P1B XA847 static display at Farnborough on 5 September 1994. This aircraft was first flown on 4 April 1957 and used by CFE in early 1958. It was withdrawn from use in 1966 after braking trials at Farnborough, having flown 205 hours and allocated to RAF Museum at Hendon in 1972, but was replaced by a Lightning F.6 in April 1988. (*Philip Birtles*)

Work then started rapidly to improve engine and warning system integrity, which proved satisfactory by the end of October 1959. The first P1B was used mainly for handling and performance development and it was joined by the fourth prototype XA853, which was first flown by Des de Villiers on 5 September1957. This aircraft was mainly allocated to Aden gun firing trials based at Boscombe Down. XA847 was fitted with the first stage larger fin by May 1958, and showed a marked improvement, particularly in rapid roll, allowing expansion of the high-speed boundary towards Mach 2. Although the RAF requirement was for M 1.7 with the Lightning Mk.1, the increased speed capability was a company project looking into future developments. The first trial to Mach 2 was scheduled on 12 December 1958, flying XA847 at 40,000 feet with a good weather forecast over the Irish Sea. Flying due south to avoid sonic boom over land, Mach 2 was achieved off the Cumbria coast and as the aircraft decelerated, a turn was made over the South Wales coast and then returned to Warton. The Lightning had therefore caught up with the Mach 2 American F-104 Starfighter and the French Mirage development was progressing the same way, which was expected to result in possible official RAF interest.

Following its Mach 2 testing, XA847 was flown on detail aerodynamic development which was completed by mid-1959. It was then allocated to future aerodynamic

P1B XA853 carrying aerodynamic Firestreak air-to-air missiles in 1958. This aircraft was first flown on 5 September 1957 and last flown on 3 May 1963 after 153 hours 25 Minutes. It was struck off charge on 10 February 1965 and dismantled for ground testing. (*BAE Systems*)

Above: P1B XA853 underside with a pair of dummy Firestreaks and a black cockpit painted on the underside to 'confuse' an enemy. This aircraft was used mainly on weapons trials. (*Philip Birtles collection*)

Below: The third P1B XA856 which was first flown on 3 January 1958 from Warton by R. Beamont. It was delivered to Rolls-Royce at Hucknall on 24 March 1958 for Avon engine development, where it made 296 flights before being struck off charge in June 1967. (*PHTG collection via Vic Flintham*)

P1B, probably XA853, carrying a pair of dummy Firestreaks, but no ventral fuel tank is fitted. (*Philip Birtles collection*)

improvements planned for later Lightning marks. This included a long ventral tank with double capacity and provision for gun or reconnaissance equipment in the forward part of the tank. XA847 was also fitted with a dry-link flight refuelling probe, which following successful installation and trials, was fitted to the first F.1A XM169. The 5th prototype, P1B XA856, was first flown on 3 January 1958 and after handling and performance clearance, was delivered to Rolls-Royce in March 1958 for Avon development.

The pre-production batch of Lightnings was used for systems development, improving engine reliability and the major task of proving the weapons system and the integration of the Ferranti AI 23B Airpass radar. The wide-ranging autopilot featured auto-ILS approach up to Mach 2 and full auto-attack capability. For these tasks, aircraft were allocated to the contractors involved and proven by comprehensive service testing and A&AEE Boscombe Down and the other establishments. The twenty pre-production batch included XG307–XG313 and XG325–XG337, and although the aircraft specification differed little, the first three had a smaller fin, which was increased by around 30 per cent from XG310. The XG307 flew on 3 April 1958; it was to be used for flight envelope clearance and modified with the Lightning F.3 weapons system in 1961 and for auto attack trials from 1963 to 1965. XG308 flew on 16 May 1958 and was initially used for a USAF evaluation before taking part in CA trials at Boscombe. Following this, it was allocated to stalling and spinning development both from Warton and Boscombe Down.

The first aircraft to be allocated to missile development was XG309, which first flew on 23 June 1958 and used for Firestreak loading and jettisoning trials in 1959. This continued at Boscombe in 1960, before it was allocated to Red Top development. Flown on 17 July 1958, XG310 was converted to the F.3 prototype with a flat top fin in 1961 and assessed for handling at Boscombe in 1962. It was used for stalling, spinning and roll clearance when carrying Red Top missiles from 1963 to 1964. The next aircraft allocated to weapons development was XG312 which flew on 29 December 1958 and was used on Airpass development for the next two years by Ferranti based at Bitteswell. It was then converted to F.3 standard and continued Airpass trials from 1962 to 1964. The first Lightning to join missile development at Hatfield was XG325 which flew on 26 February 1959 and was based with the de Havilland Propeller Company from 1962. It was joined by XG329, which flew on 30 April 1959 and used on Red Top testing in 1962/63. Red Top development was continued with XG332, which flew on 29 May 1959 until it crashed spectacularly on approach to Hatfield on 13 September 1962, with the pilot successfully ejecting.

The flight line at Warton on a snowy winter's day with the first three development Lightning F.1s. Roland Beamont is at the base of the ladder on the right with three of his colleagues. It was rare for test flying to be delayed due to weather because of the beneficial effect of the Gulf Stream. (*BAE Systems*)

Above: First pre-production Lightning F.1 XG307 being flown for the first time by R. P. Beamont from Samlesbury on 3 April 1958. It was delivered to A&AEE Boscombe Down on 24 February 1964 where it was used for service trials. It ended up on the RAE Bedford dump in July 1971. (*Philip Birtles collection*)

Below: Lightning F.1 XG308 was first flown on 16 May 1958 and after trials at Warton was delivered to RAE Bedford on 6 April 1966. It ended up on the fire dump there by April 1972. (*BAE Systems*)

Above: Lightning F.1 XG311 fitted with the smaller fin and carrying dummy Firestreaks. This aircraft was first flown on 20 October 1958 and was used for tropical trials in Aden from July to October 1961. It was successfully abandoned on 31 July 1963 when the undercarriage failed to lower and crashed in the sea off Warton after a total of 238 flying hours. (*Gordon Willams*)

Below: Lightning F.1 XG312 on the flight line at Warton during a cold day. This aircraft was first flown on 29 December 1958 and was mainly based at Bitteswell for Ferranti radar development. It last flew on 12 October 1966, when the windscreen failed at M 0.9 and 37,000 feet. The aircraft landed safely, but was not flown again having achieved 303 hours 53 minutes. The aircraft went to Shoeburyness and was struck off charge in April 1972. (*BAE Systems*)

Above: Lightning F.1 XG325 at Hatfield with de Havilland Propellers for Red Top development. This aircraft was first flown on 26 February 1959 and was finally struck off charge at Warton in March 1966 after flying 221 hours 2 minutes. It went to Shoeburyness on 28 October 1968. (*Garry Lakin collection*)

Below: Lightning F.1 XG329 at Hatfield in June 1966 used for Red Top development. This aircraft was first flown on 30 April 1959 and was based at Hatfield from 6 April to 21 December 1966. (*Philip Birtles*)

Above: Lightning F.1 XG329 at the Cranwell Engineering School on 16 October 1970, where it had been delivered as 8050M. (*Philip Birtles*)

Below: Lightning F.1 XG332 nose close-up carrying a Red Top missile. (*BAE Systems*)

Lightning F.1 XG332 on static display at Farnborough was first flown on 29 May 1959. It was allocated to de Havilland Propellers for Firestreak and Red Top missile development, and is famous for being photographed on approach to Hatfield when the pilot, George Aird, made a low-level ejection on 13 September 1962. The cause was a fire in the rear fuselage, and the pilot, who was injured as his parachute did not have time to open, was flying again within a year. Total flight time was 138 hours 52 minutes. (*Alan Sinfield*)

Going back to systems development was among the duties allocated to XG311 which was flown on 11 October 1958 and was used for engineering trials and tropical trials in Aden. It was abandoned over the Ribble Estuary on 31 July 1963 when the undercarriage failed to function correctly. Mk.1 XG313 flew on 2 February 1959 and was used for CG handling followed by rocket firing, jettisoning and handling at Boscombe. XG326 flew on 14 March 1959 and was used for Firestreak and weapon systems sighting trials at Boscombe from 1961 until 1963. The tenth pre-production Lightning XG327 flew on 10 April 1959 and was used on weapon system development. XG328 flew on 18 June 1959 and was used for some Firestreak handling in 1960/61 as well as auto attack from 1964 until 1966. Mk.1 XG330 flew on 20 June 1959 and was used for systems and autopilot development. Lightning XG331 flew on 14 May 1959 and was allocated to engineering and operational reliability trials and then Airpass development, followed by joint weapon system trials 1964/65. Mk.1 XG333 flew on 26 September 1959 and did more hot weather trials in Aden in 1961. It was used for gun firing and radar assessment at Boscombe in 1962.

With the later aircraft in the pre-production batch more representative of the production F.1s, XG334 flew 14 July 1959 and went to the Central Fighter Establishment (CFE), but was abandoned off the East Coast on 5 March 1960 following an undercarriage malfunction. XG335 flew on 7 August 1959 and was delivered on 23 December 1959 to Coltishall for CFE assessment. It was used on

Above: Lightning F.1 XG313 firing a salvo of unguided rockets from the internal rocket pack. This aircraft was first flown on 2 February 1959 and went to A&AEE Boscombe Down on 28 June 1965 for 2-inch rocket firing trials. It was flown from Boscombe Down to Airwork at Sydenham on 25 April 1968, bringing its total flight time to 351 hours 17 minutes and became G27-115 for ground instruction in Saudi Arabia. (*BAE Systems*)

Below: Lightning F.1 XG327 at RAE Bedford on 10 November 1971. (*Philip Birtles*)

Above: Lightning F.1 XG330 was first flown on 30 June 1959 and was used for OR946 development and fire zone trials. It is pictured here on the Warton flight line with a number of development aircraft. It last flew on 5 January 1965 after 170 hours 24 minutes and was sold for scrap. (*BAE Systems*)

Below: Lightning F.1 XG331 was first flown on 14 May 1959 and was used for tropical trials in Aden during July 1960. It was retired to Shoeburyness in July 1968, having flown 196 hours 14 minutes. (*PHTG collection via Vic Flintham*)

Lightning F.1 XG333 was first flown on 26 September 1959 and was used for flight trials in Aden from July to October 1961. It has a rather rudimentary shade from the sun over the cockpit. (*PHTG collection via Vic Flintham*)

weapons systems trials from 1960 until 1963 before going on Red Top trials at Boscombe, where it crashed on 11 January 1965. XG336 flew on 25 August 1959 and also went to the CFE in 1960, followed by weapons trials from 1960 to 1966. The final pre-production Lightning was XG337, which flew on 5 September 1959 and was used for Boscombe Down assessments in 1960 and Red Top evaluation at Boscombe from 1963 to 1966.

This development batch was used widely to ensure the early Lightnings had a smooth and quick entry to service. Their systems were gradually developed as they were produced, bringing improved reliability at the start of service. The initial production batch was for twenty Lightning F.1s: XM134–XM147 and XM163–XM168, although XM168 never flew and was retained at Warton for structural testing. By 1960, acceptance testing had been achieved on the first production F.1 XM134 at Boscome Down. It joined XM135, XM136, XM137 and XM138 at the CFE at Coltishall to prepare for entry into service with the RAF, where it was welcomed with great enthusiasm. The aircraft were used by the Air Fighting Development Squadron (AFDS) for operational evaluation, to provide information to the operational pilots as the squadrons formed.

Above: Lightning F.1 XG335 B AFDS during assembly at Samlesbury. (*BAE Systems*)

Below: Lightning F.1 XG335 B AFDS was first flown on 7 August 1959 and was delivered to the AFDS at Coltishall in March 1960. It went to A&AEE on 12 November 1962 and crashed on the Larkhill ranges after an undercarriage malfunction on 11 January 1965 with a total flight time of 204 hours 26 minutes. The pilot ejected safely. (*Philip Birtles collection*)

Above: A pair of AFDS Lightning F.1s XG336 and XG335. (*Air Ministry*)

Below: Lightning F.1 XG337 in open storage at RAE Bedford on 10 November 1971. It was first flown on 5 September 1959 and was used on Red Top development fitted with F.3 fin at Warton and Boscombe Down. It was moved from Bedford to Cosford as 8056M and later to Halton. (*Philip Birtles*)

3

Lightning Development

As the Lightning F.1s were about to enter service with the RAF, development continued to transform the aircraft from a Mach 2 research aircraft into an operational interceptor. Although some provisions had been made for operational equipment in the original design, it was totally inadequate for the new weapon systems under development. The aircraft was not designed for easy maintenance in service, with access often limited, sometimes requiring an engine to be taken out to reach a small component. The engines and their compartments had a tendency to leak flammable fluids onto the hot jet pipe of the lower engine. This often resulted in a catastrophic fire burning through control lines with a corresponding loss of control and the need for the pilot to abandon the stricken aircraft. Future developments were designed to overcome many of the shortcomings, usually with success, although the ground crew had to learn how to blindly wire lock bolts.

One major modification considered was fitting a jettisonable Napier Double Scorpion rocket motor in the ventral pack to boost the Lightning to high altitude to meet incoming hostile bombers. When the threat changed to low level, this requirement was cancelled.

The priority was to increase the inadequate endurance offered by the internal fuel plus the 250-gallon ventral tank, by fitting a flight refuelling probe. This was introduced on the production line with XM169, which was the first of the second batch of thirty aircraft, although only twenty-eight were built. This aircraft became the first F.1A which was flown from Samlesbury on 16 August 1960 with the probe fitted under the port wing. This version was fitted with a UHF radio, in addition to internal changes to equipment and cables, resulting in an external fairing along the lower fuselage. This initial F.1A was retained at Warton for flight refuelling trials until delivery to 111 Squadron on 14 October 1964.

The next Lightning version was the F.2 and forty-four were ordered with the serials XN723–XN735 and XN767–XN797. XN723 flew on 11 July 1961 and was delivered to Boscombe Down for service trials. It then went to Rolls-Royce for engine development, but like a number of other Lightnings, crashed due to a fire in number 2 Avon with the pilot using his ejection seat. Externally there was little to differentiate from the F.1A, but the Avon 210s were fitted with a fully variable reheat system, and the pilot benefitted from an offset TACAN (Tactical Navigation) system, improved flight instrumentation and a liquid oxygen breathing system.

Production Lightning F.1A XM171 was first flown on 20 September 1960 and delivered to Boscombe Down on 10 November 1960. It then joined 56 Squadron at Wattisham on 28 February 1961, followed by 226 OCU. It was retired to 60 MU on 11 September 1973, from where it was struck off charge on 25 March 1974. (*BAE Systems*)

The next single-seat Lightning was the F.3, a more effective second-generation Lightning, allowing more modern avionics and weapons to be introduced. Power was double that of the P.1A with Avon 300 engines developing 13,500lb dry thrust, increased to 16,000lb with reheat. The Red Top all-aspect IR air-to-air missiles allowed a head-on interception which also featured an improved Airpass airborne interception radar designated AI 23B. No Aden cannons were fitted to this version, which was limiting for the pilot who had no offensive capability left after the missiles had been launched. A gun-armed fighter pilot could at least put a warning shot across the nose of an intruder, which could not be achieved with a missile. This omission was addressed with the later F.6 when cannons could again be fitted. Red Top had a greater range than Firestreak and was faster. It was also larger, resulting in an increased fin area of 15 per cent, recognised by a flat top to the fin. Although there was a small increase in internal fuel, this was more than used up by the more powerful Avons, still limiting the endurance without regular flight refuelling, which allowed longer patrols or deployments.

The prototype F.3 was a conversion of one of the pre-production batch, XG310, flying on 16 June 1962, followed by XG327 which was the first to be modified to full F.3 aerodynamic configuration. Another four of the pre-production batch,

XG328, XG329, XG331 and XG332 were also used for F.3 development, with the last two allocated to Red Top trials with de Havilland Propellers at Hatfield. The first production F.3 XP693, was later modified to F.3A and XP694 was allocated to Ferranti for AI 23 development, before being eventually delivered to 29 Squadron. The first F.3 delivered to the RAF, XP695 was delivered to the CFE on 1 January 1964. With orders for seventy F.3s, it was the highest number of any mark, with serials XP693–XP708, XP735–XP765, XR711–XR728 and XR747–XR751 built, and many later modified to interim F.3/F.6 configuration, with others to the full F.6 standard. The F.3 was a much more capable interceptor with an advanced weapons system, but a lack of range was still a limiting factor, although that was about to be improved.

With the realisation that the Lightning was not going to be the last RAF manned fighter following the 1957 Defence White Paper, funds were made available to improve the fuel capacity along the lines promoted by the manufacturer. A new, larger capacity ventral fuel tank was developed by the Warton design team and fitted with a pair of fins to maintain directional stability, which was fitted to XP697. It also featured the earlier tested, but not adopted, more efficient cambered wing leading-edge extension. This helped increase the range by 20 per cent with little performance penalty. Wing area increased by around 13 square feet and lift was improved at high angles of attack. The modifications improved overall range and high-altitude performance, particularly subsonic speeds. Handling in the circuit was improved, particularly at low power. The minor disadvantages were slightly higher stick forces on take-off and landing and slower rolling response. Range was further increased by fitting a pair of 260-gallon overwing fuel tanks for long range

Lightning F.1 XG327 fitted with an F.3 fin and a camera fairing under the cockpit. This aircraft was first flown on 10 April 1959 and was used for radar trials until conversion to F.3 standard and was flown from RAE Bedford for supersonic noise testing. It was stored in August 1971 and went to St Athan for ground instruction mid-1972 as 8188M. It was last noted at the Manston Fire School in 1981. (*BAE Systems*)

Above: Lightning F.1 XG329 was first flown on 30 April 1959 and mainly used for weapons development. (*BAE Systems*)

Below: Lightning F.1 XG332 during Red Top trials. (*BAE Systems*)

First production Lightning F.3 XP693 at Boscombe Down on 19 March 1971 fitted with the 30mm cannon tank installation used on the later F.6s. It was first flown on 16 June 1962 and later converted to F.3A configuration. It was originally delivered to Boscombe Down on 1 November 1967 and continued on gun trials at Boscombe Down and Warton. (*Philip Birtles*)

deployments; the pylons also being adaptable for additional weapons carriage. Underwing tanks were not an option due to the main undercarriage installation. The larger ventral tank and overwing tanks, none of which were jettisonable, brought the total fuel capacity to over 1,000 gallons. This concept was so attractive to the RAF, who ordered a range of improvements both in the fuel system and weapons systems designated initially F.3A, but later became the ultimate F.6.

The first F.3A/F.6 was XP693 converted from an F.3 and was flown on 17 April 1964. Among other things, it was used to check the aerodynamic effects of the ventral weapons pack loaded with 2-inch rockets. In addition to a pair of F.2s, XN724 and XN725 were also converted. XN725 was powered by Avon 301s, featured the new wing shape and had been initially converted to F.3 standard. It was used to develop the ventral tanks, and later used for a comprehensive programme of experimental flying. The initial batch of sixteen F.6s XR752–XR767 did not have provision for overwing fuel tanks and did not feature some of the systems modifications. XR752 was flown from Samlesbury on 16 June 1965 and was delivered to the CFE at Binbrook on 26 November, joining XR753 for RAF assessment. Out of sixteen Interim F.6s, fifteen were later modified to full standard F.6s, the exception being XR766 which crashed in the North Sea on 7 September 1967 after take-off from Leuchars—the pilot ejecting successfully. The first of thirty-nine fully equipped F.6s, XR768 was delivered to 74 Squadron on 1 August 1966, the serials being XR768–XR773, XS893–XS904 and XS918–XS938.

At the Farnborough Air Show in 1962, a Lightning was shown with the new ventral tank and optional weapons pack, suggesting a potential ground attack capability. Although the RAF was not interested in this capability, it was included to make the Lightning more attractive for export. Naval and swing-wing projects were also studied but not pursued.

Above: Lightning F3/6 XP697 at Farnborough in September 1966 fitted with the export under wing 2-inch rocket pods for BAC testing. This aircraft was first flown on 18 July 1963. It was finally used for static testing at Warton in 1981. (*Philip Birtles*)

Below: Prototype Lightning F.3 XN725 used for the development of the overwing fuel tanks and enlarged ventral fuel tank. It was first flown on 31 March 1962 and later served at RAE Bedford. (*BAE Systems*)

Above: Roland Beamont in the cockpit of Red Top armed Lightning F.3 prototype XN725. (*BAE Systems*)

Below: Prototype Lightning F.3 XN725 with overwing fuel tanks and with the cambered wing leading edge. (*BAE Systems*)

The last single-seat Lightning version to enter service with the RAF was the F.2A, which featured most of the F.6 improvements including an enlarged ventral fuel tank, cambered wing, larger fin and airfield arrester hook. It was not stressed for carriage of the overwing tanks. In addition to the two 30mm cannon guns in the upper nose, it had the revised gun pack in the forward section of the ventral tank. This version was first shown publicly at the Farnborough Air Show in 1970 and XN733 was fully modified with four Aden cannons. Out of the forty-four F.2s built, thirty-two were modified to the F.2A configuration starting with XN795, although it retained the original wing planform and was used for development flying including Tornado 27mm Mauser gun trials.

The other twelve F.2s remained unconverted, of which BAC bought five for the Saudi contract, two were used for F.3 trials, and two were lost in crashes. The other three remained as F.2s with the RAF and used as target facilities aircraft for 19 and 92 Squadrons.

It was only when BAC revealed the multirole Lightning F.53 that an interest began from overseas, despite the lack of interest by the RAF. The RAF were only interested in guided missiles and 30mm cannons, but the provision of pylons in the overwing and underwing positions allowed rocket packs to be installed giving a secondary ground attack capability. This resulted in eventual orders from Saudi Arabia and Kuwait. Flight trials proved weapons could be released at all speeds, and even 1,000lb bombs could be carried. The extra weapons load had no effect on aircraft handling.

To be more effective in defending against nuclear attack, the American nuclear warhead AIR-2A Genie was considered in the late 1950s and would have been more effective against overwhelming hostile formations, than the single point attack individual air-to-air missiles. However, this project was cancelled in the early 1960s.

Lightning F.2A first development conversion XN795 was first flown as an F.2 on 30 May 1963 and was delivered to 33 MU before returning to Warton for conversion. Only the fin and ventral tank were modified and it was delivered to Boscombe Down on 12 November 1968. It returned to Warton in 1972 to support MRCA development with 27mm Mauser gun trials until 1982. (*BAE Systems*)

Above: Lightning F.2A XN733 at Farnborough on 8 September 1970 with a range of armament. It first flew as an F.2 on 1 February 1962 and was delivered to 92 Squadron on 6 June 1963. After conversion to F.2A configuration, it rejoined 92 Squadron in December 1969. It finally became maintenance airframe 8520M. (*Philip Birtles*)

Below: Lightning F.2A XN795 at Boscombe Down on 19 March 1971. (*Philip Birtles*)

Above: Early production Lightning F.6 XR754 flying over the Blackpool Tower, close to Warton airfield. (*BAE Systems*)

Below: Lightning F.6 XP693 with overwing tanks and carrying the markings of 65 (R) Squadron, although it never served with an RAF squadron. After conversion to F.6 configuration it was used by BAC in support of many trials programmes. On retirement in December 1992 it was bought by the Lightning Flying Club as G-FSIX on 22 December and moved to Exeter. It was later acquired by Thunder City in Cape Town and is now owned by Ian Black, who keeps it stored at Binbrook. (*BAE Systems*)

4

Two-seat Lightnings

The most obvious change to the Lightning was the production of the two-seat advanced trainer. Although the two-seat version was not available from the start, it was obviously desirable for new pilots being introduced to such an advanced and demanding Mach 2 fighter. Plans were initially made from 1957 for a dual-control operational trainer, not just for handling, but also for mastering the weapons systems. This version was originally designated P11, and the initial version was based on the Lightning F.1A. The instructor and student were sat side-by-side allowing not just use as a dual-control pilot trainer, but also having full operational capability. Although the overall length of the aircraft was not changed, the forward single-seat cockpit was replaced by a two-seat re-profiled nose to accommodate two Martin Baker 4BST ejection seats, which increased the overall width by 11.5 inches (30cm). There was no effect on performance as the cannons had been removed saving weight, and the new nose shape helped to conform with the drag-reducing 'Area Rule'. The prototype was built in production jigs with the new nose and in addition to full dual-pilot control, was equipped with all the weapons systems, including a pair of Firestreak air-to-air missiles. If used operationally, the two-seat version could be flown by a pilot and the weapons systems the responsibility of the second crew member.

Roland Beamont flew the first two-seat Lightning XL628 from Warton on 6 May 1959 and during the 30-minute flight comfortably exceeded Mach 1. This aircraft was flown at the 1959 Farnborough Air Show where, for the first time, it was revealed as Lightning T.4 titled below the cockpit and was carrying a pair of Firestreaks. Not long after, on 1 October when being flown by Johnny Squier, the fin broke off after a roll at high altitude in excess of Mach 1. The aircraft was over the Irish Sea, and control was lost so quickly that the pilot was unable to put out a distress call. This was the first ejection above Mach 1, but the seat separated at 10,000 feet and the pilot descended by parachute into the uninviting waters below. Despite seeing rescue aircraft around him, and releasing distress flares, he was not spotted and finally managed to paddle ashore exhausted, using pieces of driftwood and was picked up from the unwelcome experience.

The aircraft had only flown nearly 41 hours in ninety-four flights during its short career, but the second prototype, XL629 had flown on 29 September and took over the bulk of the early flight development programme. However, on 19 November, when flown by Beamont and de Villiers, the canopy came off during the take-off run

Above: Lightning T.4 prototype XL628 landing at Warton on 6 May 1959 after first flight by R Beamont with brake chute and air brakes deployed in natural metal finish. No ventral fuel tank was fitted. (*BAE Systems*)

Below: Lightning T.4 prototype XL628 with yellow training bands around rear fuselage and wings. A ventral fuel tank has been fitted to give greater endurance. (*BAE Systems*)

Lightning T.4 prototype XL628 at Farnborough in September 1959 carrying a dummy Fireflash and a smart colour scheme. This aircraft crashed in the Irish Sea on 1 October 1959. (*Philip Birtles*)

of XL629. The departure was abandoned without any injuries to the crew, or further damage to the aircraft. After use for flight development, including handling, stability, stalling and spinning, XL629 was delivered to the ETPS at Farnborough on 13 May 1966, moving to Boscombe Down on 20 December 1967. It was retired in 1975 and is on static display at the airfield.

A batch of twenty T.4s XM966–XM974 and XM987–XM997 was ordered for the RAF, with the first flown by Beamont from Samlesbury on 15 July 1960. It was later converted at Filton to the second T.5 configuration. Like the prototype, it suffered fin failure over the Irish Sea on a test flight on 22 July 1965 and was abandoned successfully by the two pilots, who were rescued much more quickly than Johnny Squire. The RAF took delivery of eighteen T.4s for 226 Operational Conversion Unit (OCU) with front line squadrons for currency checks and instrument ratings. Two were later bought back by BAC for Saudi Arabia.

The T.5 was based on the F.3 and recognisable by the flat-top fin. A total of twenty-two (XS416–XS423, XS449–XS460 and XV328–XV329) were ordered, with the XL417 first flown on 20 August 1964. These aircraft replaced T.4s with the OCU and front line squadrons, plus the LTF (Lightning Training Flight) at Binbrook. The original order had been for twenty T.5s, the additional two replacing two earlier T.5s, the first XS453, which had crashed on 1 June 1966. The second one replaced was XS460, which was bought back by BAC as the first T.55 trainer for Saudi Arabia.

Above: Second prototype Lightning T.4 XL629 which first flew on 29 September 1959. (*BAE Systems*)

Below: Second prototype Lightning T.4 XL629 at Boscombe Down on 19 March 1971. It was flown at A&AEE from June 1961 on general handling trials including stall and spinning development. It went to the ETPS at Farnborough from 13 May 1966 and moved to Boscombe Down on 20 December 1967. It was withdrawn from use on 3 November 1975 and pole mounted by the ETPS HQ in 1982. (*Philip Birtles*)

Above: Production Lightning T.4 XM974 in the static park at Farnborough in September1961. This aircraft first flew on 19 June 1961 and was delivered to 74 Squadron on 3 August 1962. It crashed into the North Sea on 14 December 1972 due to engine fires, and both pilots ejected safely. (*Philip Birtles*).

Below: Lightning T.4 two pilot cockpit. (*BAE Systems*)

Above: Converted to first T.5 at Filton XM967 was first flown 30 March 1962. It was delivered to RAE Farnborough on 22 May 1968. (*BAE Systems*)

Below: Lightning T.5 XM967 prototype conversion was allocated as maintenance airframe 8433M at the RAF Colerne Museum, where it was up for disposal on 27 July 1975 and relegated to the Kemble fire dump by December 1976. (*Philip Birtles*)

5

Lightning Joins the RAF

RAF evaluation started with three CFE pilots based at Warton, making sixteen flights between 17 January and 3 March 1958. The aircraft offered were the original P1A WG760 fitted with the cambered wing leading edge, the first P1B XA847 and the third XA856. P.1B XA847 was flown the most with thirteen sorties, six of which were pilot familiarisation and seven flight profiles. XA847 was flown with and without the ventral fuel tank at all with weights of up to 30,900lb and achieved Mach 1.5. With a high level of enthusiasm building for the new interceptor, three late aircraft from the pre-production batch, XG334–XG336 were delivered to the CFE at Coltishall in December 1959.

The first production F.1 XM134 was flown Samlesbury to Warton on 3 October 1959 and after company flight trials, was delivered to A&AEE Boscombe Down on 31 March 1960 for pre-service evaluation. It then went to AFDS at Coltishall in July, where it was used in the early stages of developing air combat capability at speeds up to Mach 2.

The service evaluation was allocated to the Air Fighting Development Squadron (AFDS), the task being to establish operational parameters for service pilots. The runway at Coltishall had been lengthened, among other improvements to the station, for Lightning operations and the front line unit to be designated to introduce this potent aircraft to regular RAF service was 74 Squadron, flying Hunters from the same base. The first F.1 of twelve to be delivered to 74 Squadron was XM165 on 29 June 1960, accompanied by four AFDS aircraft returning from a successful air defence exercise based at Leconfield.

Out of the production batch of twenty F.1s, XM134 to XM168, nineteen were flown by 74 Squadron, only the last one XM168 not serving, as it became a non-flying structural airframe. XM134 returned to Warton for development flying on 10 November 1960 before rejoining 74 Squadron on 2 September 1963. However, it had to be abandoned with control difficulties on 11 September 1964 with the wreck falling in the Wash. The wreckage was recovered for an accident investigation at the AIB Farnborough, where the cause was found to be a fire in the rear fuselage which had burned through the tail controls.

Following service with the CFE at Coltishall, XM135 and XM136 joined 74 Squadron. XM135 went to 226 OCU in September 1963 and Leuchars TFF before retirement to 60 MU on 28 June 1971. XM136 also went to 226 OCU in

September 1964, before allocation to Wattisham TFF in August 1966. It was lost on 13 September 1967 following loss of control with a reheat fire in the rear fuselage. XM137 and XM138 both served with CFE before joining 74 Squadron. XM137 joined 74 Squadron on 2 October 1962, then 226 OCU in September 1964. It served with Binbrook, Leuchars and Wattisham TFFs until retiring to 60 MU at Leconfield in November 1973. XM138 joined 74 Squadron but suffered a fire on landing at Coltishall on 16 December 1960 and was relegated to fire practice in October 1966. XM139 was the first to be delivered by an RAF service pilot to 74 Squadron on 2 August 1960. It went to 226 OCU in September 1964 and later served with Leuchars and Wattisham TFFs. After having a wing change at Warton, it returned to Wattisham on 19 February 1970 and was allocated as the RAF Fighter Display aircraft flown by Flight Lieutenant R. Pengelly at a number of airshows, including Farnborough in 1970 and 1972, and Paris in 1971. It was allocated to ground instruction at Wattisham in 1981 as 8411M.

The next of seven F.1s delivered in 1960 to 74 Squadron started with XM140 which arrived on 2 August and joined 226 OCU in September 1963 and then 111 Squadron as a high-speed target in January 1965, before being reduced to spares at 33 MU in October 1966. XM141 was delivered to 74 Squadron on 29 August 1960 and moved to 226 OCU where it was damaged in a take-off accident on 16 May 1961 and reduced to spares at 33 MU by August 1966. XM142 was delivered to 74 Squadron on 30 August 1960 but was abandoned successfully on 26 April 1963 off Cromer due to control failure. XM143 was delivered to 74 Squadron on 15 September 1960 before going to 226 OCU in September 1963 and reduced to spares at 33 MU in August 1966. XM144 led a bit more active life—it was delivered to 74 Squadron on 30 September 1960, then to Leconfield, Wattisham and Leuchars TFFs, finally allocated 8417M as gate guard at Leuchars. XM145 was delivered to 74 Squadron on 14 May 1962, later operating with 226 OCU and Leuchars TFF before retiring to 60 MU. XM146 was

Lightning XM139 modified to F.1A at Le Bourget on 6 June 1971. It was flown by Fl Lt R Pengelly as the RAF Fighter Display Aircraft at Farnborough in September 1970 and 1972, with Paris Show in June 1971, as well as at many other air displays. It was used for ground instruction at Wattisham as 8411M from 1981. (*Philip Birtles*)

delivered to 74 Squadron on 4 September 1960, passed to 226 OCU in September 1963 and was used by 111 Squadron as a high-speed target before being scrapped at 33 MU in November 1966. XM147 started off with AFDS on 3 September 1960 before issue to 74 Squadron. It was used by 56 Squadron, Binbrook, Wattisham and Leuchars TFFs before becoming ground instruction airframe 8412M. XM163 was initially delivered to AFDS on 4 November 1960 before going to 74 Squadron in June 1961. It went to 226 OCU in September 1964, followed by Wattisham TFF in August 1968 before retirement to 60 MU on 16 February 1972. XM164 was delivered to 74 Squadron in August 1960, then 226 OCU in September 1964. On 22 February 1964, it joined Fighter Command Trials Unit which became Binbrook TFF and was finally retired to 60 MU in April 1972. XM165 was the first delivery to the RAF when it joined 74 Squadron on 29 June 1960. It moved to 226 OCU in October 1963 and was scrapped at 33 MU in October 1966. Similarly, XM166 was delivered to 74 Squadron on 2 August 1960 and served with 226 OCU from September 1963 until scrapped at 33 MU in October 1966. The final flying F.1 was XM167 was delivered to 74 Squadron on 26 September 1960, served with 226 OCU and was withdrawn to 33 MU in October 1966.

Responsibility for introducing the Lightning to regular RAF service was with 74 Squadron, testing the operational capabilities and tactics. Losses of this totally new concept were surprisingly low, the main problem being control difficulties caused by fires in the rear fuselage. The Avon engine configuration was not ideal, with the top one prone to leak fuel and hydraulic fluid onto the hot jet pipe of the engine below, particularly in an operational aircraft. Considerable effort was made in later Lightnings to reduce leakage and protect the lower Avon. Following service with 74 Squadron, many of the F.1s went on to serve with 226 OCU, teaching new pilots

Lightning F.1s XM167 H and XM163 Q with 74 Squadron at Leuchars. XM163 was first flown on 23 April 1960 and after service with AFDS was delivered to 74 Squadron in June 1961. It went to 226 OCU in September 1964 and then Wattisham TFF, before retiring to 60 MU on 16 February 1972. XM167 was first flown on 14 July 1960 as the last completed F.1 and was delivered to 74 Squadron on 26 September 1960. It later served with 226 OCU and was struck off charge at 33 MU in October 1966 (*Garry Lakin collection*)

Above: Lightning F.1s XM143 A and XM146 L with 74 Squadron carrying Firestreak missiles overflying Leuchars. XM143 was first flown on 27 February 1960 and delivered to 74 Squadron on 15 September 1960. It served with 226 OCU and was reduced to spares at 33 MU in August 1966. (*Garry Lakin collection*)

Below: Lightning F.1 XM140 M 74 Squadron low flypast at Leuchars carrying Firestreak. It was first flown on 25 January 1960 and delivered to 74 Squadron o 2 August 1960. It served with 226 UCU from September 1963, and then 111 Squadron from January 1965, before being reduced to spares at 33 MU from October 1966. (*Garry Lakin collection*)

Above: Six 74 Squadron Lightning F.1s lined up at what may be Boscombe Down headed by XM139 C. This aircraft was first flown on 12 January 1960 and delivered to 74 Squadron on 2 August 1960. It later joined Wattisham from 19 February 1970 to become official RAF Fighter Display Aircraft, see 05.08. (*BAE Systems*)

Below: Lightning F.1 XM165 F 74 Squadron was first flown on 30 May 1960 and was the first F.1 to enter squadron service with the RAF on 29 June 1960. It went to 226 OCU in October 1963 and was scrapped at 33 MU from October 1966. (*BAE Systems*)

Above: Lightning F.1 XM145 on a maximum reheat engine run at night. This aircraft was first flown on 18 March 1960 and delivered to 74 Squadron on 14 May 1962. It was operated by 226 OCU and Leuchars TFF from September 1966 and then stored at 60 MU until mid 1973. (*BAE Systems*)

Below: Lightning F.1 XM140 M 74 Squadron carrying Firestreak at Farnborough in September1960. It was first flown on 25 January 1960 and was delivered to 74 Squadron on 2 August 1960. It went to 226 OCU in September 1963 and 111 Squadron in January 1965. It was reduced to spares at 33 MU from October 1966. (*PHTG collection via Vic Flintham*)

how to operate the aircraft and then a number served as high-speed targets for the regular squadron pilots. The F.1s were certainly challenging for the ground crew, especially in the early days when the type was being introduced to service.

Conversion from the Hunters began immediately by the Lightning Conversion Unit (LCU) with CFE pilots. Their aim was to train pilots to fly an aircraft with double the speed of the Hunter and at that time, no two-seat Lightnings were available. As an introduction, the trainee pilot would fly in formation with a Hunter flown by an experienced Lightning pilot, which would have a 28,000-foot start, to allow the two aircraft to format at operational altitude. The new pilot not only had to learn how to fly the Lightning, but also operate its weapon systems of two Firestreak air-to-air missiles and two Aden cannons, four of which were fitted to the Hunters. The de Havilland Firestreak used passive infrared guidance, which after firing, was boosted to supersonic speed by its rocket motor, locking on to the heat source until impacting with the target. The Ferranti AI 23 had radar mounted in the nose cone in the Lightning air intake, which assisted the pilot in finding the target. Once located, the pilot then selected 'lock-on', allowing target tracking automatically and guiding the pilot to within missile range of the target. The AI radar could compensate for target evasion, and when the target was within range, the missile seeker head locked on and instructed the pilot to fire.

Although the Lightning presented an understandable challenge to the air and ground crews with the squadron, the batch of twelve aircraft, plus one reserve, were delivered mostly between July and August 1960 with the twelfth on 26 September. Bad weather and low serviceability kept utilisation low initially, but over 100 flying hours were achieved in January 1961 for the first time, although a four 74 Squadron Lightning formation had flown on the Farnborough Air Show public days in September 1960. For the maintenance engineers, the Lightning was a massive step forward in technology and capability. Not only were much of the airframe and engines systems difficult to access, the radar, weapons systems and electronics were far in advance of the Hunter, which many of them had supported in the past. Achieving 100 flying hours in the month of January, in poor weather, was a major achievement. During the same month, the role of the squadron was changed from a short-range day fighter unit to the more appropriate night and all-weather fighter squadron. In April 1961, the squadron successfully participated in Exercise Matador credited with ten 'kills'.

Initially, pilots selected to fly Lightnings required 1,000 hours or over on fast jets, but it was not long before graduates from advanced flying training schools with around 50 hours fast jet experience, were posted onto Lightning front line squadrons, where they would continue to receive training to bring them up to operational standard.

Those pilots converting from the uncomplicated Hunter, required specialist training in preparation for flying the new aircraft. It usually started with a five-day aeromedical course, where the trainees were taught how to deal with high-altitude flying. All of the pilots were fitted with special flying clothing and equipment, including a pressure helmet. Lectures at the ground school included knowledge of aircraft systems, handling characteristics, navigation challenges and emergency procedures. Cockpit instrumentation and procedures were demonstrated on the basic Lightning simulator, preparing for the first solo on type. The RAF, at last, had an interceptor which could outperform the USAF Century series fighters, which had been dominant for a number of years in larger numbers.

By the time of the Farnborough Air Show in 1961, 74 Squadron replaced the previous year's four Lightning formation with nine aircraft and in 1962 became an RAF Fighter Command aerobatic team under the leadership of Squadron Leader Peter Botterill. Named 'The Tigers', the aircraft were painted in a special colour scheme, featuring the tiger emblem. Although the Lightning was not ideal for formation aerobatics, speed was limited to 400 knots to allow the formation to stay within view of the audience at most airfields, allowing turning manoeuvres, which could be contrasted with spectacular climbs and changes in altitude. In 1962, when 92 Squadron was operating a formation of overall blue Hunters as the official RAF Aerobatic Team, they combined with 74 Squadron Lightnings to achieve a composite formation display with sixteen Hunters and ten Lightnings at the Farnborough Air Show. Meanwhile, in addition to their formation skills, the 74 Squadron pilots still had to maintain an operational capability. 74 Squadron was the only squadron to operate the Lightning F.1s, which it did until April 1964, when replacement began with the more effective F.3s.

A formation of four 74 Squadron Lightning F.1s which was formed for the display season in 1960 (*BAE Systems*)

Above: Lightning F.1 XM146 L 74 Squadron at Farnborough Air Show in September 1961 before the formation of The Tigers. This aircraft was first flown on 29 March 1960 and delivered to 74 Squadron on 4 September 1960. It went to 226 OCU in September 1963 and then 111 Squadron. It was scrapped at 33 MU in November 1966. (*Adrian Balch*)

Right: 74 Squadron diamond nine Lightning F.1s XM139, 140, 142, 147, 164, 165, 166, 167 and 146, which was the official RAF Aerobatic Team for 1962, known as 'The Tigers'. (*BAE Systems*)

Above: Lightning F.1 XM165 F 74 Squadron at Farnborough Air Show in September 1962 in The Tigers colours. (*Adrian Balch*)

Below: Lightning T.4 XM974 T 74 Squadron at Leuchars in 'The Tigers' colours after its appearance at Farnborough in September 1961. (*BAE Systems*)

Lightning F.1 XM137 74 Squadron in 'The Tigers' colours carrying Firestreaks. This aircraft was first flown on 14 December 1959 and went to CFE before delivery to 74 Squadron on 2 October 1962. It went on to be operated by 226 OCU and the TFFs of Binbrook, Leuchars and Wattisham before going to 60 MU Leconfield 20 July 1974 for storage tests, having flown 766 hours and 25 minutes. (*J. J. Halley*)

While working up with the F.1s, 74 Squadron achieved a very high standard of efficiency, which was demonstrated on 23 March 1963 when Fighter Command was called to readiness at 15.02 hrs. The squadron had two Lightnings at immediate readiness, and scrambled eight F.1s in the next 2.5 hours. This was 80 per cent of available serviceable aircraft and a great credit to the air and ground crews who brought so many advanced technology aircraft to maturity in such a short time. On 26 April, total control failure was experienced in XM142 off Cromer, and Flight Lieutenant T. J. Burns made a perfect ejection without any injuries and was rapidly recovered from the sea, showing a very high level of competence from all involved.

With the F.1s coming due for replacement, the first seven departed to join T.4s with 226 Operational Conversion Unit (OCU) in July 1963 at Middleton St George. They were prepared for their training duties at 60 MU Leconfield on the way north with the red and white markings of 145(R) Squadron. The aircraft were replaced with F.1s from the AFDS, which included the first production aircraft, XM134, which also later joined the OCU.

74 Squadron moved to Leuchars on 2 March 1964 to re-equip with Lightning F.3s. Meanwhile, 226 OCU moved to Coltishall the previous month, with additional Lightnings coming from other front line squadrons as they re-equipped with later marks. Surplus aircraft were transferred to 33 MU at Lyneham, which was in the process of closing down, and they had responsibility passing of some to 60 MU at Leconfield, scrapping the remainder.

There was a requirement for realistic target aircraft in the continuing operational training of Lightning squadron pilots. The 85 Squadron Binbrook-based Canberras provided a target facilities flight (TFF) and could only operate up to 45,000 feet. Despite generating a poor radar signal, the Lightnings provided a potential answer. With priority given to re-equipping the front line squadrons, new aircraft could not be made available, but there was a plentiful supply of low hours F.1s and F.1As. In 1966, work began on converting some of these early aircraft at 33 MU following trials at the AFDS. This unit was renamed Fighter Command Trials Unit on 31 January and two F.1s XM164 and XM137 were successfully evaluated at Binbrook. With the evaluation completed, both aircraft remained at Binbrook as the TFF, followed by TFFs forming at Wattisham and Leuchars, where they were independent units from the resident squadrons with their own pilots and ground crews. The role was to simulate high-speed targets, replicating all levels of manoeuvres and deception, providing realistic threats to the squadron pilots. Each flight adopted its own markings, usually incorporating the station badge. These early Lightnings were popular with pilots, as their task was just to fly the aircraft without carrying the extra weight and challenges of weapons systems, and the aircraft were often selected for individual aerobatic displays, using up hours on non-operational aircraft.

It was at 33 MU that the commanding officer made an unplanned Lightning flight on 2 July 1966. The pilot was 40-year-old engineering officer, Wing Commander Walter 'Taffy' Holden in XM135 and the aircraft was being prepared for supersonic target duties with Fighter Command.

Lightning F.1A XM181 with the Binbrook TFF. It was first flown on 25 January 1961 and was delivered to 111 Squadron on 29 September 1961. It was with 56 Squadron in May 1963 and ended up as 8415M at Binbrook. (*Peter March*)

Above: Lightning F.1A XM144 B Wattisham TFF at Binbrook 16 October 1969. This aircraft was first flown on 14 March 1960 and was delivered to 74 Squadron on 30 September 1960. After service with Wattisham TFF it went to Leuchars TFF and finally became 8417M as gate guard at Leuchars from 1981. (*Philip Birtles*)

Below: Lightning F.1A XM147 with the Wattisham TFF in 16 September 1972. This aircraft was first flown on 7 April 1960 and was delivered to AFDS on 3 September 1960, before going to 74 Squadron. It then was used by 56 Squadron and Wattisham TFF, before becoming instructional airframe 8412M. (*Philip Birtles*)

Lightning F.1A XM177 Wattisham TFF touching down on the Farnborough runway on 10 September 1972. This aircraft first flew as an F.1A on 20 December 1960 and was delivered to 56 Squadron on 28 February 1961. It was flown by 226 OCU and Wattisham TFF, before being broken up at 60 MU in March 1974. (*Philip Birtles*)

On the first test flight by a Boscombe Down test pilot, a stand-by inverter warning came on just after take-off. Despite a full investigation, no fault could be found, but it was repeated on the next two flights. The decision was then made to isolate the two inverter parts and test them separately by taxi tests. As the Boscombe pilot was unavailable, Holden was briefed on the maximum rpm which the brakes could restrain and advised him of cockpit precautions. He went through full cockpit checks and went over the full engine running procedures before XM135 was towed to the runway. The cockpit canopy was removed to allow additional test wiring to be installed, the ejection seat was disarmed with safety pins in place and the undercarriage

Lightning F.1A XM135 with Leuchars TFF. This aircraft ended up preserved at IWM Duxford. (*Adrian Balch collection*)

ground locks fitted. As the fault had appeared on all three occasions, the plan was to increase engine power between 80 and 90 per cent of full power, held back by the brakes, release them and immediately pull back on power and stop the aircraft.

Positioned at the end of runway 18/36, Holden was strapped in, ready for cockpit checks. The engines were started and with three test runs made, there was adequate runway for a fourth attempt. On the fourth run, Holden inadvertently pushed into reheat resulting in immediate acceleration of the aircraft; he thought the throttles had jammed. By the time he realised this was not the case, speed was increasing rapidly, only 2,000 feet of runway remained, which was insufficient to stop—his only choice was to take-off. Without any functioning radio communications, ATC fortunately guessed what was happening and alerted the emergency services.

Unable to eject, the Wing Commander had no alternative but to attempt to land. He had little flying experience, which amounted to solo in a Harvard many years before and a flight in a Javelin T.3 in November 1962, when he had not made a landing or take-off. He carefully made a circuit to approach runway 07, but the first three attempts failed to achieve a good approach position; he had particular difficulty keeping the power setting correct. He decided to take advantage of the 12kt wind at 20 degrees and changed his approach to runway 25 and the first attempt failed due to high speed and altitude, but on the second attempt an arrival was made, nose high at 160kt. The tail-skid hit the runway hard, damaging the tail parachute release mechanism; it fell away when deployed. By heavy braking on the slightly uphill runway, Holden was able to stop the aircraft with about 100 yards left to run, after 12 minutes' flight time. The ex-74 Squadron aircraft was repaired and issued to the TFF at Leuchars and Station Flight at 60 MU before being retired to the IWM at Duxford on 20 November 1974, with 1,343 flying hours, where it is now preserved.

With the availability of Lightning F1As off the Samlesbury production line, the next RAF front line fighter units could re-equip. The first of these was 56 Squadron at Wattisham, with XM172 delivered on 14 December 1960, followed by five more Lightnings by June, which allowed training and working up to progress. There was a period of training at Coltishall, while the runway at Wattisham was prepared for full Lightning operations. With the F.1As fitted with a flight refuelling probe, endurance was improved, but not really overcome until the F.6 with its larger ventral fuel tank. Therefore, 56 Squadron was tasked with intensive flight refuelling trials, which included two aircraft making the first overseas Lightning flight to Akrotiri in Cyprus on 23 July 1962, with a non-stop flight taking 4 hours 22 minutes. Fuel was provided by 90 and 214 Squadrons Valiant tankers. This led to confidence for four 56 Squadron Lightnings to make the 2,000-mile flight to Cyprus as a routine training task for the average squadron pilot, with four different squadron pilots flying the return trip. This laid the foundations for all Lightning squadron pilots to learn flight refuelling techniques, which would be used during their training for deployments overseas as far as Singapore.

The next famous long-serving RAF unit to re-equip with Lightning F.1As was 111 Squadron, which not only served with distinction in the Battle of Britain, introducing Hurricanes into service, but also as the 'Black Arrows' RAF aerobatic

Above: Lightning F.1As of 56 Squadron lined up at Wattisham in 1962. (*PHTG collection via Vic Flintham*)

Below: Lightning F.1A XM173 V 56 Squadron at Coltishall in 1961 carrying Firestreak. This aircraft was first flown on 1 November 1960 and delivered to 56 Squadron on 2 January 1961. It became 8414M as gate guardian at Bentley Priory in 1981. (*PHTG collection via Vic Flintham*)

Above: Lightning F.1A XM179 S 56 Squadron with 'Firebird' markings in line up at Wattisham. This aircraft was first flown on 4 January 1961 and was delivered to 56 Squadron on 28 February 1961. Mid-air collision on 6 June 1963 with XM171 and pilot ejected, but was seriously injured. (*Garry Lakin collection*)

Below: Lightnings of 56 Squadron 'Firebirds' lined up at Wattisham in March 1963, headed by T.4 XM989 X. This aircraft was first flown on 30 August 1962 and delivered to 56 Squadron on 5 September 1962. It was bought back by BAC for the Saudi Arabia contract as T.54 54-650 on 6 April 1966. (*Adrian Balch*)

Above: Lightning F.1As diamond nine of 56 Squadron Firebirds practising near Wattisham in March 1963. (*Adrian Balch collection*)

Below: Five Lightning F.1As of 56 Squadron Firebirds practising in 1963. (*PHTG collection via Vic Flintham*)

Above: Lightning F.1A XM171 A 56 Squadron carrying a pair of Firestreak air-to-air missiles. This aircraft was first flown on 29 September 1960 and initially went to Boscombe Down on 10 November 1960. It was delivered to 56 Squadron on 28 February 1961 and collided mid air with XM179 6 June 1963, but landed safely and was repaired. It served with 226 OCU, then to 60 MU on 11 September 1973 and was struck off charge on 25 March 1974. (*PHTG collection via Vic Flintham*)

Below: Lightning F.1A XM174 D 56 Squadron at Wattisham ready to taxi out for take-off carrying Firestreak missiles in 1963. This aircraft was first flown on 15 November 1960 and delivered to 56 Squadron on 15 December 1960. It was operated by 226 OCU and Leuchars TFF, but crashed during approach to Leuchars on 29 November 1968, and the pilot ejected safely. (*PHTG collection via Vic Flintham*)

Above: Lightning F.1A XM179 J 56 Squadron Firebirds taxiing in at Wattisham carrying Firestreaks. (*BAE Systems*)

Below: Lightning T.4 XM989 X 56 Squadron. (*PHTG collection via Vic Flintham*)

team with its 22 Hunter spectacular loops. Its first F.1As XM184 and XM186 were delivered to 111 Squadron at Wattisham on 13 April 1961. Training started immediately with the aim of becoming operational as soon as possible, including flight refuelling and overseas trials in Germany, Malta and Cyprus. There were nine Lightnings with 111 Squadron by the end of June 1961, although one—on loan from 56 Squadron, XM185, had been abandoned by its pilot due to undercarriage problems on 28 June. The squadron was declared fully operational by 29 September, with just six months conversion from the subsonic Hunter to the Mach 2 Lightning. During October, the squadron aircraft were grounded due to the need to lag and separate all closely routed hydraulic pipes to avoid some of the fire risk.

In 1963, 56 Squadron was declared the Fighter Command aerobatic team, replacing 92 Squadron, which was to replace its Hunters with Lightning F.2s. Known as the 'Firebirds', the squadron continued the tradition of a special colour scheme with red fin, fuselage spine and wing leading edges featuring the Phoenix squadron identity. Their otherwise successful season was marred by the loss of XM174 and XM179, which collided during a practice over Wattisham. Flight Lieutenant Mike Cook ejected from XM179, but during the process, his neck was broken and he was paralysed, confined to a wheelchair. XM174 landed safely at Wattisham. For the 1964 season, 56 Squadron remained the Fighter Command aerobatic team, replaced by 111 Squadron 'Treble One' in 1965 with twelve F.3s.

Line astern formation of five 111 Squadron Lightning F.1As with XM215 C at rear. This aircraft was first flown on 11 July 1961 and was delivered to 111 Squadron on 2 August 1961. It later served with 226 OCU and Binbrook TFF before being allocated to ground instruction as 8421M in 1981. (*PHTG collection via Vic Flintham*)

Above: Lightning F.1A XM191 H 111 Squadron at Bentwaters open day on 11 May 1963. This aircraft was first flown on 8 May 1961 and delivered to 111 Squadron on 28 June 1961. It was destroyed at Wattisham on 9 June 1964 after a fire in the rear fuselage and the pilot, who was uninjured, managed to land back at base. (*Philip Birtles*)

Below: Lightning F.1A XM216 P 111 Squadron at Coltishall. This was the last F.1A to fly and was delivered to 111 Squadron on 29 August 1961. It was operated by 226 OCU and became 8426M in 1981. (*Philip Birtles collection*)

Above: Lightning T.5 XS450 T 111 Squadron at Wattisham on 5 August 1967 as part of the squadron jubilee celebration. This aircraft was first flown on 25 May 1965 and was delivered to 111 Squadron on 6 September 1965. It became 8534M at Binbrook by 1981. (*Philip Birtles*)

Below: Lightning F.1A XM184 A 111 Squadron in full 'Black Arrows' markings. This aircraft was first flown on 9 February 1961 and was delivered to 111 Squadron on 13 April 1961. It was written off when it caught fire while landing at Coltishall on 17 April 1967. (*PHTG collection via Vic Flintham*)

Lightning T.4 XM992 Z 111 Squadron on the flight line at Wattisham in Black Arrows markings. This aircraft was first flown on 13 December 1961 and delivered to 111 Squadron on 24 September 1962. It was bought back by BAC for the Saudi contract on 7 April 1966, and was delivered on 6 June 1966 as T.54 54-651. (*J. J. Halley*)

The two Wattisham squadrons worked closely together, including 111 Squadron training in ground attack, to investigate the suitability of the Lightning in this role. The squadron sent detachments to the El Adam ranges in Libya, where in addition to air-to-air firing the 30mm cannons, 2-inch rocket packs replaced the Firestreaks, as well as air-to-air gunnery with the cannons. Apart from one firing made at Mach 1.4 from 48,000 feet, most were made from 36,000 feet at Mach 0.95. On all occasions, cannons were fired from ventral packs, apart from one occasion when all four cannons were fired. To maintain reasonable sortie periods, flight refuelling was essential, not only from RAF tankers, but also Fleet Air Arm Sea Vixens fitted with an underwing buddy pack.

With the three Lightning F.1/F.1A squadrons proving the concept of a Mach 2 fighter in the battlefield, it fell to 19 and 92 Squadrons to introduce the Lightning F.2 to active service. 19 Squadron had introduced the Spitfire into RAF service ready for the Second World War. 19 Squadron had moved to Leconfield on 29 June 1959 with Hunter F.6s, which it began preparing for conversion to Lightning F.2s in December 1962 with the delivery of T.4 XM988 on 29 October. The first T.4 was followed by three more T.4s, XM994, XM995 and XM972 by 15 November. The first F.2 XN775 arrived at Leconfield on 17 December and on its acceptance flight on 10 January 1963, it was found to have a fault in the reheat. On the previous day, F.2 XN778 had to make a precautionary diversion to Finningley with a fire warning indicated during an air test. Despite these minor delays, the squadron had twelve F.2s and a T.4 by March, by which time it had been declared operational. The F.2 benefited from a fully variable reheat and improved instrumentation over the F.1A. During July, 19 Squadron flew 280 sorties with a total of 216.30 hours, and by October, 375 sorties in over 300 hours was reached and this included ninety-eight practice supersonic interceptions. As with the earlier squadrons, flight refuelling was essential and the 19 Squadron F.2s had a detachable probe under the port wing with training starting in January 1964.

Above: Line up of 19 Squadron Lightning F.2s at Gutersloh on 23 September 1965 with T.4 XM991 T heading the line. This aircraft was first flown on 4 October 1961 and was initially delivered to 226 OCU at Middleton St George before joining 19 Squadron. It was damaged at Gutersloh on 3 May 1974 and as a result allocated the maintenance number 8456M. (*PHTG collection via Vic Flintham*)

Below: Lightning F.2 XN774 C 19 Squadron carrying Firestreak missiles. It was first flown on 27 September 1962 and delivered to 19 Squadron on 13 February 1963. It was converted to an F.2A at Warton on 13 August 1969 and finally became 8551M. (*Garry Lakin collection*)

Above: Lightning F.2 XN727 A 19 Squadron at Akrotiri around mid 1964. It was first flown on 13 October 1961 and delivered to 19 Squadron at Leconfield. It was converted to a F.2A in 1969 and ended up at Farnborough as 8547M in 1977. (*PHTG collection via Vic Flintham*)

Below: Lightning F.2 XN778 F 19 Squadron was first flown on 9 November 1962 and delivered to 19 Squadron on 9 January 1962. It was converted to an F.2A, delivered to 92 Squadron on 19 December 1968 and finally became 8537M. (*PHTG collection via Vic Flintham*)

Above: Lightning F.2 XN787 M 19 Squadron was first flown on 15 February 1963 and delivered to 19 Squadron on 22 March 1963. It went to Warton on 1 July 1969 for conversion to F.2A after which it was delivered to 92 Squadron. It was stored at 60 MU in July 1973 and became 8522M. (*PHTG collection via Vic Flintham*)

Below: Lightning T.4 XM991 T 19 Squadron on finals to land at Gutersloh. This aircraft was first flown on 4 October 1961 and delivered initially to 226 OCU at Middleton St George. It then went to 19 Squadron, but was damaged at Gutersloh on 3 May 1974 and became 8456M. (*BAE Systems*)

Lightning T.4 XM973 V 19 Squadron at Gutersloh in olive finish. This aircraft was first flown on 17 May 1961 and was delivered to 74 Squadron at Coltishall on 3 August 1962. It then served with 19 Squadron and was finally allocated maintenance serial 8528M. (*Garry Lakin collection*)

The 19 Squadron Lightnings were tasked with air defence of UK airspace and maintained a pair of F.2s on Quick Reaction Alert (QRA) close to the end of the duty runway, ready for a rapid take-off in the event of the approach being detected of a potential hostile aircraft. In June 1964, 19 Squadron used their flight refuelling skills on a deployment to Cyprus. In 1965, the squadron participated in flight refuelling trials with the Victor K.1 tankers, which replaced the premature retirement of the Valiants due to metal fatigue.

To complete the Leconfield Lightning Wing, 92 Squadron formed in April 1963, although in preparation, the first Lightning F.2 XN727 was delivered on 23 January. This aircraft, together with an T.4 was used to start conversion of the pilots from Hunters. Most of the remaining F.2s were delivered starting at the end of March, followed by six more in April, bringing the squadron to full strength by the end of June, allowing the unit to become fully operational before the end of the summer. Following a flight refuelling exercise, XN785 crashed on 27 April while attempting to land in an emergency at disused Hutton Cranswick, unfortunately killing the pilot.

Carrying on the tradition of the earlier Lightning squadrons, 92 became the RAF aerobatic team for 1964, and appeared at the Farnborough Air Show, among many other displays. Despite their aerobatic display responsibilities, 92 Squadron still had to maintain its training schedule along with 19 Squadron, mainly on developing the ground attack capability, using the four-cannon armament. This was in addition to their air defence role; the ground attack being in preparation for both squadrons posting to Germany.

Above: Lightning F.2 XN783 A 92 Squadron landing at Leconfield. This aircraft was first flown on 26 January 1963 and was delivered to 92 Squadron. It was converted to F.2A from 16 November 1969 and then delivered to 19 Squadron. It became 8526M. (*Garry Lakin collection*)

Below: Lightning F.2 XN728 B 92 Squadron was first flown on 26 October 1961 and was delivered to 92 Squadron on 1 April 1963. It was converted to F.2A and returned to 92 Squadron on 24 June 1969, later becoming 8546M. (*PHTG collection via Vic Flintham*)

Lightning T.4 XM968 Q 92 Squadron heading a line-up of F.2As XN782 H and XN775 B at Gutersloh. This aircraft was first flown on 9 November 1960 and operated by 226 OCU and 56 Squadron before joining 92 Squadron, finally allocated 8541M. (*BAE Systems*)

The first unit to be moved to Germany was 19 Squadron to Gutersloh on 23 September 1965; it was the first supersonic aircraft to join the 2nd Tactical Air Force (2nd TAF). This was followed by 92 Squadron to Geilenkirchen on 29 December. Both squadrons were integrated into the defence of Northwest Europe, with their air defence role consisting of round-the-clock QRA, as well as perfecting their ground attack capabilities. The Lightning F.2 was voted the most popular mark by the pilots, especially those who had experienced earlier versions, although the aircraft still suffered fuel and hydraulic leaks.

Line up at Leconfield of 92 and 19 Squadrons Lightning F.2s on 30 July 1963. This was also the home for 60 MU. (*PHTG collection via Vic Flintham*)

Above: Lightning F.2A XN791 B 19 Squadron on finals to Gutersloh on 20 June 1969. This aircraft was first flown on 4 April 1963 and delivered to 19 Squadron on 15 May 1963. It went to Warton on 21 March 1968 for conversion to F.2A and was delivered to 92 Squadron on 29 October 1968. It was finally allocated 8524M. (*John Mounce*)

Below: Lightning F.2A XN735 A 19 Squadron at Gutersloh on 20 June 1969. This aircraft was first flown on 23 February 1962 and delivered to 92 Squadron on 10 May 1963. It was delivered to Warton on 30 August 1968 for conversion to F.2A and then delivered to 19 Squadron at Gutersloh on 25 April 1969. It was finally allocated 8552M. (*John Mounce*)

Lightning F.2A XN781 B 19 Squadron in olive finish fitted with large ventral fuel tank. This aircraft was first flown on 12 December 1962 and delivered to 19 Squadron at Leconfield on 15 March 1963. It went to Warton on 13 September 1966 for conversion to F.2A and returned to 19 Squadron 26 February 1968. It was finally allocated 8538M. (*Garry Lakin collection*)

On 24 January 1968, 92 Squadron made the obvious move to join 19 Squadron at Gutersloh, bringing all support, logistics and training to one base, which was located only 80 miles from the West German/East German border, making reaction time very short in times of tension. The further improved F.2A, with many similar features to the F.3/6 Lightnings, including large ventral tank and flat top fin, began to arrive with 19 Squadron in the form of XN789 on 15 January 1968, followed by 92 Squadron in August. The F.2s were progressively returned to the manufacturer for conversion to the new standard and of the forty-four F.2s built, twenty-eight were converted to F.2As for the two Gutersloh units. The F.2A was lighter than the F.6, making it easier to handle, and was even more popular with the pilots.

Echelon of four Lightning F.2s with XN768 nearest over Germany in 1967. This aircraft was first flown on 14 March 1962 and was delivered to 92 Squadron in May 1973. It was not converted to F.2A and ended up on Gutersloh dump in September 1973 as 8347M. (*PHTG collection via Vic Flintham*)

Above: Line up of 92 Squadron Lightning F.2s at Leconfield with XN793 K nearest. This aircraft was first flown on 1 May 1963 and was delivered to 92 Squadron on 21 June 1963. It went to Warton on 26 September 1968 for conversion to F.2A and returned to 9 Squadron at Gutersloh on 1 May 1969. It was damaged at Gutersloh on 18 September 1973 and allocated 8544M. (*BAE Systems*)

Below: Lightning F.2A XN775 B 92 Squadron on finals to Gutersloh on 20 June 1969. This aircraft was first flown on 1 October 1962 and was the first to enter RAF service when it was delivered to 19 Squadron on 17 December 1962. It was delivered to Warton on 7 June 1968 for conversion to F.2A and joined 92 Squadron on 15 January 1969. It was finally allocated 8448M. (*John Mounce*)

Above: Lightning F.2A XN774 F 92 Squadron on approach to Gutersloh in olive finish. This aircraft was first flown on 27 September 1962 and was delivered to 19 Squadron on 13 February 1963. It went to Warton on 13 August 1969 for conversion to F.2A after which it was delivered to 92 Squadron. It was finally 8551M. (*Garry Lakin collection*)

Below: Lightning F.2As XN730 J olive finish and XN793 A natural metal finish 92 Squadron over Germany. XN730 was first flown on 23 November 1961 and was delivered to 19 Squadron on 12 March 1963. It was converted to F.2A and delivered to 92 Squadron on 30 August 1968, and finally became 8496M. (*BAE Systems*)

Being located so close to the 'Iron Curtain' border with East Germany, both Gutersloh based squadrons could react much quicker than other NATO defences with their QRA rapid reaction interceptor role. Two Lightning F.2As were able to make a rapid scramble from purpose-built hangars near the active runway, in what was known in NATO as the Interceptor Alert Force. To maintain this state of readiness, both the pilots and ground crews rehearsed for threats under all anticipated conditions, including nuclear and chemical attacks. One of the major challenges was unservicability due to poor provisioning of spares for the Lightning fleet, with fuel leaks being a major problem; some airframe parts were also in short supply. The front line Germany-based squadrons were the worst affected, with some aircraft being cannibalised for parts to keep the front line operational. There were times during 1971 and early 1972 when only around 50 per cent of Lightnings were available, with priority given to the QRA aircraft. Much of the problem with non-availability of vital parts was caused by insufficient funding following on from the major cuts in the 1957 Defence White Paper, which had never increased enough to support eight squadrons of Lightnings providing front line defence of Britain and NATO. Fortunately, spares availability gradually improved, which was assisted by the tremendous efforts of dedicated ground crews. Despite these difficulties, all operational tasks were met or exceeded and at times over 500 sorties per month were being achieved.

It was clear from the start of Lightning development that a two-seat conversion trainer would be required to prepare Hunter pilots for the vastly increased performance of the new fighter. Even experienced pilots found the early methods of training unsatisfactory when the early F.1s entered service. The arrival of the first T.4 XM970, which was first flown on 5 May 1961, was delivered to the Lightning Conversion Squadron (LCS) at Middleton St George on 2 November. It was taken on charge of what was to become 226 OCU on 27 June 1962. When the unit moved to Coltishall in 1964, Middleton St George became a civil airport for the northeast of England. The basic strength of the OCU was ten T.4s, with the addition later of some F.1As for continuation training. The OCU adopted the identity of 145(R) Squadron to be available for combat in times of hostility, flown by instructors. The instructors would fly both versions of the Lightning in Fighter Command exercises to ensure that they remained operationally current. With the T.4, first tour pilots could graduate from flying training schools on to Lightnings, the successful graduates completing some 60 hours at the OCU on both T.4s and F.1As before being posted to an operational squadron. Their training would continue over a number of months on how to operate the Lightning as a weapon system, before they were declared operational.

With the earlier versions of the Lightning being replaced by the F.3, there was a need for a more representative trainer, resulting in the complimentary T.5 being developed; the first XS419 was delivered to Coltishall on 20 April 1965. Both trainers were fully operational and were issued to squadrons to maintain currency standards and be used for renewal of instrument ratings. In May 1971, the initial student training role consisting of basic handling techniques on F.1As and T.4s was designated as 65(R) Squadron with appropriate markings on the aircraft front fuselage. Once they had completed the early phase of the training, the students then went on to the T.5s of the advanced 145(R) Squadron. This part of the OCU also trained weapons' instructors who were already qualified to fly the aircraft.

Above: Lightning T.4 XM988 226 OCU at Coltishall on 7 November 1961 seen from the fire gate as it passed by on the perimeter track. This aircraft was first flown on 21 August 1961 and delivered to 226 OCU at Middleton St George on 12 October 1962. It crashed into the North Sea on 5 June 1973 and the pilot ejected safely. (*Philip Birtles*)

Below: Lightning F.1A XM215 226 OCU attended the Tiger Meet at Woodbridge on 7 August 1969 with the Union Jack on the fin. (*Philip Birtles*)

Above: Lightning T.4 XM974 226 OCU departing Wattisham on 24 April 1968. (*Philip Birtles*)

Below: Lightning T.4 XM969 226 OCU at the Tiger Meet at Woodbridge on 7 August 1969 on finals to land. This aircraft was first flown on 28 March 1961 and was delivered to 226 OCU at Middleton St George mid-1961. It was finally burned on the Binbrook fire dump in 1982. (*Philip Birtles*)

Above: Lightning F.3 XR716 at Leconfield on 25 July 1970. This aircraft was first flown on 19 November 1964 and was delivered to 111 Squadron on 4 February 1965. After service with 226 OCU, it went to 5 Squadron at Binbrook and was withdrawn from use by 1983. (*Philip Birtles*)

Below: Lightning T.5 XS458 226 OCU at Woodbridge on 7 August 1969. This aircraft was first flown on 3 December 1965 and was delivered to 226 OCU at Coltishall on 2 February 1966. It had joined 11 Squadron at Binbrook by 1983. (*Philip Birtles*)

Lightning T.5 XS458 in a special 226 OCU livery. (*Garry Lakin*)

The next version of the Lightning to enter service with the RAF was the more effective F.3. After a protracted development period, the first XP695 was delivered to the AFDS at Binbrook on 1 January 1964. The second XP696 arrived two weeks later and the last two of the four allocated to the AFDS, XP749 and XP750 had been delivered by April. Service trials continued with the AFDS being renamed the Fighter Command Trials Unit in February 1966, by which time only two F.3s remained and departed soon after.

The first delivery to an active unit was F.3 XP700, which was issued to 74 Squadron at Leuchars in April 1964, and adopted as the commanding officer's mount coded A. By July, the F.1s had all been replaced by F.3s, sharing the air base with 23 Squadron Javelins, which converted to Lightning F.3s from August 1964, crewed mainly by experienced Lightning pilots from the other squadrons. The first pair of F.3s, XP707 and XP708 was delivered to Leuchars on 19 August 1964. Sadly, on 28 August 1964 XP704 crashed during a practice aerobatic display for the Battle of Britain show the following month, killing the pilot, Flight Lieutenant Owen, with many of the station personnel watching. Both Leuchars squadrons were declared operational on the F.3 by early 1965, taking turns with northern ORP duties. Training inflight refuelling was still a priority as the F.3 had little significant endurance increase over the earlier versions. Much of the early flight refuelling training was from USAFE KC-135 using their wing-mounted hose and drogue system, as the Valiants were withdrawn in 1964 due to fatigue cracking, pending the conversion of Victor B.1s to tankers in 1965. Once the Victor K.1s were based at Marham, they were kept available to top up the fuel for Lightnings on interception duties investigating UK airspace intrusions, training or deployment overseas. The Lightnings on ORP duties were busy defending British airspace against Soviet reconnaissance aircraft, gathering data and testing our air defences, particularly off the north of Scotland. The plan was to intercept the hostile aircraft around 250 miles from our coast, keeping the Leuchars squadrons busy, and requiring flight refuelling while following the intruders.

Above: Lightning F.3s XP751 B and XP702 C 74 Squadron. XP751 was flown on 16 March 1964 was the first F.3 delivered for service with the RAF. It later went to 111, 29 and 5 Squadrons. (*Crown Copyright*)

Below: Lightning F.3 XP700 A 74 Squadron at Leuchars on 19 September 1964. This aircraft was first flown on 6 June 1963 and delivered to 74 Squadron on 14 April 1964. It joined 29 Squadron in July 1972, but crashed on 7 August 1972 after damaging the tail skid and ventral tank on take-off. The pilot ejected safely. (*PHTG collection via Vic Flintham*)

The next two units to covert to F.3s were Wattisham-based to cover the southern QRA. 111 Squadron began to convert from December 1964, followed by 56 Squadron in March 1965, replacing F.1As. The aircraft were then polished aluminium and the squadrons began decorating the aircraft with some outstanding liveries, probably the most flamboyant being 56 Squadron with red and white checkers on the fin and the squadron Phoenix on a white disc, surrounded by a red arrowhead on the front fuselage. Other Lightning squadrons also decorated their aircraft with imaginative schemes, but they had to be toned down by the end of 1965 by official order.

Above: Lineup at Wattisham of six 111 Squadron Lightning F.3s with XP741 K heading the line. This aircraft was first flown on 4 February 1964 and was delivered to the squadron on 22 December 1964. (*Crown Copyright*)

Below: Lightning F.3 XR715 E 111 Squadron departing Wattisham on 24 April 1968. This aircraft was first flown on 14 November 1964 and delivered to 111 Squadron on 8 January 1965. It went to 29 Squadron in 1972, but crashed at Blyford Green on 13 February 1974. (*Philip Birtles*)

Above: Lightning F.3 XP754 R 111 Squadron at Coltishall on 30 July 1974. This aircraft was first flown on 5 June 1964 and was delivered to 74 Squadron on 31 July 1964. It passed to 111 Squadron in 1972. (*Philip Birtles*)

Below: Lightning T.5 XS450 T 111 Squadron in full squadron markings in December 1965. This aircraft was first flown on 25 May 1965 and delivered to 111 Squadron on 6 September 1965. (*PHTG collection via Vic Flintham*)

Above: Lightning T.5 XS450 T 111 Squadron at Wattisham on 5 August 1967 on the occasion of the Squadron's Jubilee. It eventually went to Binbrook as 8534M in 1981. (*Philip Birtles*)

Below: Lightning F.3 XR728 D 56 Squadron was first flown on 17 March 1965. It was converted to an F.6 and delivered to 23 Squadron on 1 November 1967, later being operated by 56 and 11 Squadrons. (*Garry Lakin collection*)

Above: Lightning F.3 XR714 D 56 Squadron in its red/white flamboyant livery at Lakenheath on 22 May 1965. This aircraft was first flown on 14 November 1964 and delivered to 56 Squadron on 8 January 1965, later going to Akrotiri. (*Philip Birtles*)

Below: Lightning XR718 C 56 Squadron in full Firebirds livery was first flown on 14 December 1964. It was delivered to 56 Squadron on 1 April 1965 and was later operated by 5 Squadron at Binbrook. (*Adrian Balch collection*)

Lightning F.3 XR718 C 56 Squadron in toned down markings at North Weald in June 1966. (*Philip Birtles*)

Above: Lightning T.5 XS417 Z 56 Squadron at Wattisham in 1976. (*PHTG collection via Vic Flintham*)

Below: Lightning T.5 XS459 X 56 Squadron was first flown on 18 December 1965 and later was operated by 29 Squadron and the LTF. (*Garry Lakin collection*)

In the spring of 1965, 111 Squadron formed a twelve aircraft aerobatic team with a T.5 and the remainder F.3s. They performed at a number of air shows, including one at Exeter on 26 June. During the solo display in XR712, which was Flight Lieutenant Doyle's final high speed Mach 0.92, he suffered a No. 1 engine fire with parts falling over the airfield. On the way back to St Mawgan, he had to eject and was picked up from the sea by a 22 Squadron Wessex, suffering bruising to his back. On 29 September 1965, Lightning F.3 XP739 was lost when both engines flamed out on approach to Wattisham. Flight Lieutenant H. Molland made a successful ejection without injury. The year 1966 started badly with the loss of 56 Squadron F.3 XR721, when the pilot was killed after a crash landing on approach to Bentwaters after his No.1 engine flamed out. He attempted to eject, but the canopy would not jettison and only went off when he hit obstructions during what was otherwise a successful landing; the seat ejected with the pilot receiving fatal injuries. In October 1966, 56 Squadron made a deployment to Malta for exercise ADEX 66 where it was highly successful. On 11 April, 56 Squadron was posted to Akrotiri in Cyprus as part of the RAF Near East Air Force (NEAF), sharing the base with Vulcans and Hercules, replacing 29 Squadron Javelins which began to convert to Lightning F.3s on 10 May at Wattisham. Meanwhile, 56 Squadron were busy with the Cyprus crisis in 1967. In November 1967, Turkish Cypriots took over the northern part of the Island, and invasion was threatened with support from Turkey. Great care had to be taken by 56 Squadron to avoid escalation of the situation, which remained at Akrotiri for four years until it began to replace the F.3s with the much-improved F.6s from September 1971. The Lightning F.6s were ex-74 Squadron at Tengah in Singapore which disbanded on 1 September 1971; its aircraft being flown back from Asia to equip 56 Squadron in Cyprus.

Lightning F.3 XP703 G 29 Squadron at Wattisham on 16 September 1972 was first flown on 28 September 1963. It was delivered to 74 Squadron on 8 June 1964 and went to 29 Squadron in 1972. It finished up in the MOD(PE) fleet at Warton in 1981. (*Philip Birtles*)

Above: Lightning F.3 XP743 B 29 Squadron at Wattisham on 16 September 1972 was first flown on 18 February 1964 and delivered to 33 MU on 18 February 1965. (*Philip Birtles*)

Below: Lightning F.3 XP765 A 29 Squadron on the Wattisham flight line on 16 September 1972. It was first flown on 26 September 1964 and delivered to 33 MU on 27 November 1964. It was operated by both 56 and 29 Squadrons. (*Philip Birtles*)

Above: Lightning F.3s with 29 Squadron on detachment to Akrotiri for armament practice camp. (*Philip Birtles collection*)

Below: Lightning T.5 XV328 Z 29 Squadron at Wattisham on 24 April 1968. This aircraft was a replacement for a T.5 diverted to Saudi Arabia and was first flown on 22 December 1966. It was delivered to 60 MU and then issued to 29 Squadron. It went to 5 Squadron in 1973 and was stored at Binbrook by 1983. (*Philip Birtles*)

As already mentioned, the F.3 compatible T.5 was delivered to 226 OCU, the first of twenty-two built, with twelve issued to the Coltishall based OCU and others allocated to the active squadrons. In 1972, 226 OCU was split into two squadrons, replacing 145 Squadron. 2T Squadron was equipped with Lightning F.3s and T.5s, while 65 (R) Squadron operated F.1As and T.4s.

Above: Lightning F.3 XP696 2T Squadron at Coltishall 30 September 1974 with a smart white fin and spine. This aircraft was first flown on 2 July 1963 and delivered to CFE on 15 January 1964. It was used on Red Top development at Boscombe Down from 16 February 1966 until 5 June 1967 and was delivered to 226 OCU in August 1972. (*Philip Birtles*)

Below: Lightning F.3 XP737 2T Squadron at Lakenheath on 18 August 1979 and was first flown on 1 January 1964. It was initially delivered to 23 Squadron on 21 October 1964 and was stored at Filton until issued to 226 OCU/2T Squadron. (*Philip Birtles*)

Above: Lightning T.5 XS454 at Coltishall was first flown on 6 July 1965 and delivered to Leuchars on 9 October 1965, followed by 226 OCU/2T Squadron. (*Garry Lakin collection*)

Below: Lightning F.1A XM215 226 OCU/65(R) Squadron at Upper Heyford on 12 August 1972. (*Philip Birtles*)

Above: Lightning T.4 XM970 226 OCU/65(R) Squadron at Upper Heyford on 18 June 1971. This was the first T.4 to enter RAF service and was first flown on 5 May 1961. After participating in some development flying, it was delivered to 226 OCU on 2 November 1961. (*Philip Birtles*)

Below: Lightning T.4 XM996 226 OCU/65(R) Squadron being prepared for engine runs. This aircraft was first flown on 13 April 1962 and delivered to 226 OCU on 14 January 1963. (*PHTG collection via Vic Flintham*)

During the early to mid-1970s, the Lightning air defence force reached its maximum strength in operation with eight RAF squadrons. The only departure being 74 Squadron in Singapore, which disbanded on 1 September 1971 due to the political decision to withdraw British forces from Asia. However, as already mentioned, their F.6s were passed to 56 Squadron in Cyprus to replace the earlier interim standard aircraft.

With the increasing availability of the F.6 configured Lightnings, four of the F.3-equipped units adopted F.6s, the only exception being 29 Squadron which remained with F.3s at Wattisham until 31 December 1974. The first to re-equip with F.6s was 74 Squadron in June 1966 at Leuchars in preparation for deployment to Tengah, Singapore on 12 June 1967, where it remained until September 1971. The next unit was 23 Squadron which re-equipped in May 1967 at Leuchars; they were responsible for the northern QRA. In Cyprus, 56 Squadron re-equipped with F.6s in September 1971 at Akrotiri, using ex-74 Squadron aircraft. The final unit was 111 Squadron which re-equipped in May 1974 at Wattisham for only a few months.

The Lightning Force continued to defend UK air space mainly against Cold War threats, with new pilots joining after flight training on Jet Provosts and Hawks—the latter providing some experience of weapons system operation. Following conversion at the OCU, they would be posted to the frontline squadrons where they would be introduced to flight refuelling and the secondary ground attack role, the Lightning remaining highly effective. From the mid-1970s, the replacement commenced with Phantom FGR.2s which had the advantage of a pilot and weapons systems operator,

Lightning F.6 XR727 F 23 Squadron departing Wattisham on 24 April 1968 during the celebration of Fighter and Bomber Commands into Strike Command. This aircraft was first flown on 8 March 1965 as an F.3 and converted to an F.6. It was delivered to 23 Squadron on 15 September 1967, later being operated by 11 Squadron. (*Philip Birtles*)

Above: Lightning F3/6 XR753 A 23 Squadron at Lakenheath with white fin and spine. This aircraft was first flown on 23 June 1965 and was delivered to the CFE on 16 November 1965. It served with both 5 and 23 Squadrons before modification to full F.6 at Warton from 31 January 1968 and was operated by 5 Squadron. (*Garry Lakin*)

Below: Lightning F.3/6 XR760 H 23 Squadron at Wattisham 24 April 1968. This aircraft was first flown on 20 September 1965 and delivered to 23 Squadron. It was fully modified to F.6 and delivered to 56 Squadron in January 1968 in Cyprus, and by 1981 had joined the LTF at Binbrook. (*Philip Birtles*)

the latter taking responsibility for guiding the pilot to an advantageous attack position by interpreting the interception radar and operating the ECM system.

On the front line at Gutersloh in RAF Germany, the highly effective F.2A force began winding down with the disbandment of 19 Squadron on 31 December 1976, followed by 92 Squadron on 31 March 1977. When 19 Squadron disbanded, its aircraft with adequate life remaining without a major overhaul, were transferred to 92 Squadron. The surplus was stripped for spares and many parked out on the airfield at Gutersloh as decoy targets in the event of an attack. Some of the airframes were allocated to maintenance training and remained at Gutersloh until they were finally scrapped and removed. With a reduced training requirement, 226 OCU disbanded on 30 September 1974.

Left: Lightning F.3/6 XR753 A 23 Squadron escorting a Russian Bear over the North Sea. (*BAE Systems*)

Below: Lightning T.5 XS417 Z 23 Squadron which was first flown on 17 July 1964 as the first production T.5 to fly. It was used for some development flying before delivery to 226 OCU on 25 May 1965 and then went to 23 Squadron. By 1983 it was with 11 Squadron at Binbrook. (*Garry Lakin collection*)

6

The Ultimate RAF Lightning: The F.6

The ultimate RAF Lightning was the very effective F.6. 5 Squadron was responsible for its introduction to service when it moved from operating Javelins in Germany to Binbrook on 7 October 1965, taking delivery of its first interim F.6 on 10 December. The first T.5 was delivered on 19 November, to start conversion training and familiarisation. The first two F.6s delivered were XR755 and XR756, followed soon after by XR754—all three to become long term residents at Binbrook. With production rate an average of three aircraft a month, it wasn't until 8 March 1966 before the twelfth aircraft, XR765, an interim F.3/F.6 was delivered, completing the squadron allocation. The squadron work-up was delayed by problems with raising the aircraft nose on take-off, which was solved by increasing the nose wheel oleo pressure. In February 1967, a Royal Netherlands Air Force squadron visited Binbrook with their F-104s allowing comparisons with other NATO units. While the Dutch pilots enjoyed the T.5 experience, the F-104s featured many shortcomings, despite it being widely adopted by NATO.

Lightning F.1A XM181 Y 5 Squadron at Cottesmore on 10 July 1971. This aircraft first flew on 25 January 1961 and was delivered to 111 Squadron on 29 September 1961. It went to 56 Squadron in May 1963 and later 5 Squadron while it was operating F.6s. It had a fire on engine runs at Binbrook and was allocated 8415M. (*Philip Birtles*)

Above: Lightning F.3 XR726 N 5 Squadron on the ORP at Wattisham on 24 April 1968, which was converted to F.6. This aircraft was first flown on 26 February 1965 and delivered to 60 MU on 12 July 1967. It was damaged by fire at Binbrook on 19 October 1973. (*Philip Birtles*)

Below: Lightning F.3 XR749 Q 5 Squadron at Lakenheath on18 August 1973. This aircraft was first flown on 30 April 1965 and delivered to 56 Squadron on 4 October 1967. It was operated by both 5 and 11 Squadrons. (*Philip Birtles*)

Above: Lightning F.3/6 XR755 O 5 Squadron at Benson on 14 September 1968. This aircraft was first flown on 15 July 1965 and delivered to 5 Squadron on 10 December 1965. (*Philip Birtles*)

Below: Lightning F.6 XS898 K 5 Squadron on the ORP at Wattisham on 24 April 1968. It was first flown on 20 May 1966 and delivered to 5 Squadron on 9 January 1967. (*Philip Birtles*)

Above: Lightning F.6 XS901 A 5 Squadron at Finningley on 29 July 1977 in camouflage finish carrying Red Top. This aircraft was first flown on 1 July 1966 and was delivered to 5 Squadron on 20 February 1967. It also was operated by 56 Squadron in Cyprus and 11 Squadron at Binbrook. (*Philip Birtles*)

Below: Lightning F.6 XS919 F 5 Squadron at Abingdon on 16 September 1978 with the gun pack in the forward section of the ventral fuel tank and showing the cranked wing leading edge. This aircraft was first flown on 28 September 1966 and was delivered to 11 Squadron on 14 April 1967. It also served with 56 Squadron in Cyprus and 5 Squadron at Binbrook. (*Philip Birtles*)

The USAF reduced its orders for F-104s, which could achieve Mach 2 rapidly, but was deficient in many other ways. These included failing to achieve its full operational requirements. This should have been a sign of its shortcomings but Lockheed had set up a major production line for NATO air forces, putting the Lightning in the shadows, and West Germany placed the launch order for the F-104 Starfighters in Europe, giving it credibility undeserved promotion. The British government invested too little, too late in Lightning developments and its short endurance did not help. However, by 1966, there had been sufficient investment in the Lightning programme to produce the ultimate F.6 with improved fuel capacity.

The first unit to introduce the full production standard Lightning F.6 was 74 Squadron with XR768 delivered on 1 August 1966 to Leuchars, gradually replacing the F.3s. This aircraft spent many years with 74 and later 5 Squadrons before a double engine flame out on 29 October 1974, when the pilot successful ejected off Mablethorpe. By December 1966, the full compliment of twelve F.6s had been delivered to 74 Squadron. The pilots were enthusiastic about the improved endurance, particularly with the overwing fuel tanks for overseas deployments. To prove the increased endurance, in January 1967, the squadron F.6s were flying 5-hour sorties around the UK, cruising at 35,000 feet, and coming down to top up with fuel from tankers. This was in preparation for a four Lightning trip to Cyprus in preparation for eventual deployment to Singapore in June 1967. Before departure in March, 74 Squadron tested an airfield arrester system in the event of a suspected brake failure. This consisted of a spring-loaded arrester hook fitted under the rear fuselage and lowered by the pilot to pick-up with a cable stretched across the runway 400 yards from the upwind end and was restrained hydraulically. It was known as the Rotary Hydraulic Arrester Gear with successful trials and adopted by all Lightning F.2As and F.6s.

The squadron also investigated the compatibility of the F.6 overwing tanks with Victor tankers. These trials included a minimum of two receiver sorties to investigate the flight refuelling envelope, followed by twenty-four further flight refuelling sorties on typical cross country flights. The sorties were flown from 10 to 31 March involving 96 flying hours. The trials were an overall success, with minor fuel venting, making the 74 Squadron ready for Operation Hydraulic, the deployment from Leuchars to Tengah in Singapore. However, before this the first live firing of a Red Top missile was made by a squadron pilot from a Lightning on 12 April. Unfortunately, the missile failed to perform correctly, making violent manoeuvres and fell into the sea on the Cardigan Bay ranges. A second firing from another Lightning exploded prematurely soon after launch, causing great concern since the F.6 did not at the time have cannon armament. Red Top reliability was later to improve significantly. Despite this setback, 74 Squadron departed for Singapore on 4 June with the first six aircraft led by Wing Commander Ken Goodwin heading for Cyprus as the initial staging point. Five more Lightnings followed the next day, with the final two departing on 6 June. Flight refuelling was available from 17, 55, 57 and 214 Victor BK.1 tankers, with other staging stops in the Middle East and the Island of Gan in the Indian Ocean. All thirteen Lightnings arrived at Tengah by 11 June, ready for operations the next day. Because the fuel capacity was less in the T.5 than F.6, and XV329 was prepared for shipping to Singapore, and although it suffered some minor corrosion during the voyage, it was soon repaired and issued to the squadron.

Lightning F.6 XS927 N 74 Squadron at Tengah in February 1969. This aircraft was first flown on 15 February 196 and was delivered to 74 Squadron on 3 April 1967. (*Adrian Balch collection*)

Lightning F.6 XS896 J 74 Squadron at Tengah December 1968. This aircraft was first flown on 25 April 1966 and delivered to 74 Squadron on 7 December 1966. It crashed on approach to Tengah on 12 December 1968, killing the pilot. (*Adrian Balch collection*)

Lightning F.6 XS895 H 74 Squadron in formation with XR771 and XS896 J, all carrying overwing fuel tanks. XS895 was first flown on 6 April 1966 and delivered to 74 Squadron on 5 December 1966. It also served with 56 and 5 Squadrons. (*Adrian Balch collection*)

The Lightnings were the only air defence RAF aircraft in Asia and fit well into the new environment, providing a high level of readiness. Adjustment to the new, much improved flying conditions was rapid, with a high level of serviceability achieved. In January 1968, an exercise to test the RAF and FAA capabilities was initiated with Sea Vixens from HMS Eagle providing a mock attack against the defending Lightnings. The 74 Squadron pilots had anticipated an easy 'win' but found the Sea Vixens a major challenge. The subsonic Sea Vixens approached in two pairs, one duo designated as bombers, and the other fighter escorts. The 'bombers' approached at 30,000 feet using cloud cover when available, while the fighter escort approached at 43,000 feet, leaving an identifying contrail. This required the defending Lightnings to make a choice of intercepting the high-level escort fighters, allowing the bombers to get through to the target, or they could locate the bombers and attempt to stop them.

For the 'bombers' to survive, they detected the approaching interception and turned through 90 degrees allowing the 'fighters' to descent into a quarter attack, with the Lightning to be neutralised by inferior aircraft. The high speed of the Lightning could be an embarrassment and result in overshooting the target, especially during a head on approach. As a result of the exercise, the 'bombers' were successfully intercepted on one occasion just before bomb release. During the other three simulated attacks, the bombers got through, although with the loss of the fighter escort. Lessons were learned by 74 Squadron pilots, allowing them to revise their procedures ready for an international exercise the following month.

This exercise consisted of Royal Australian Air Force (RAAF) Mirages and Sabres operating from Butterworth, together with RAF Far East Air Force (FEAF) Canberras, Hunters and Meteors. Out of a total of fifty-four interception sorties, it was estimated that some 65 per cent were destroyed before release of weapons, and in twenty-nine interceptions flown by Lightnings, thirteen Kills were claimed, one of which was a Mirage before weapon release. This demonstrated that the Lightning was superior to the Mirage in air-to-air combat and could out-manoeuvre the skilled RAAF pilots. In addition to formal exercises, the ideal flying conditions allowed the full range of combat training, including practising aerobatics and scrambles. In October 1968, 74 Squadron was able to remind the USAF they were not invulnerable at high altitude, when a pair of Tengah Lightning F.6s practice intercepted a RB.57F highly modified Canberra at an altitude where the America crew thought they were safe.

In 1969, in addition to the routine combat training, 74 Squadron was invited in June to fly four F.6s to Darwin in Northern Australia, which also included the forces of New Zealand, Singapore and Malaysia, to test the defences of the latter two countries. The Lightnings flew Combat Air Patrols (CAPs) supported by 214 Squadron Victor tankers against Canberras and Vulcans, many at night over the sea, when the lessons learned from the previous exercises were applied with success. With the British government's decision to pull out from Asia, 74 Squadron was withdrawn in August 1971 and formally disbanded on 1 September. Its aircraft were ferried to Akrotiri to replace its interim F.3/6s with fully updated F.6s.

Meanwhile in 1968, 5 Squadron made a non-stop flight to Bahrain with flight refuelling from Marham based Victor tankers. The 4,000-mile flight took 8 hours.

They also deployed to Singapore in early 1970 to join 74 Squadron in local exercises, and brought back some Lightnings in need of overhaul, leaving replacements. For their excellence in weapons proficiency, 5 Squadron won the Dacre Trophy twice and as top NATO interceptor squadron achieved the Huddleston Trophy against the combat jets from eight other countries in challenging all-weather conditions, by which

Above: Lightning F.3/6 XR763 B 11 Squadron at Upper Heyford on 28 August 1970. This aircraft was first flown on 15 October 1965 and delivered to 5 Squadron on 11 February 1966. It was brought up to full F.6 configuration and delivered to 23 Squadron on 1 November 1967, 11 Squadron in November 1973 and finally 5 Squadron. (*Philip Birtles*)

Below: Lightning F3/6 XR754 A 11 Squadron at Finningley on 29 July 1977 with ventral cannon pack and camouflaged. This aircraft was first flown on 8 July 1965 and was delivered to Boscombe Down on 3 December 1965. After modification to full F.6 standard, it was delivered to 23 Squadron, then 11 and 5 Squadrons. (*Philip Birtles*)

time the RAF was only operating the Lightning with two squadrons, the other being 11 Squadron. No. 11 Squadron had reformed at Leuchars on 3 April 1967 with F.6s beginning to arrive the same month and moved to Binbrook on 28 March 1972. When 74 Squadron went to Singapore, 11 Squadron took over their role as air defence of the UK, which continued with the move to Binbrook.

Above: Lightning F.3 XR720 M 11 Squadron in camouflage finish at Greenham Common on 31 July 1976 while the squadron was operating F.6s. This aircraft was first flown on 24 December 1964 and was delivered to 11 Squadron in December 1973, later operating with the LTF. (*Philip Birtles*)

Below: Lightning F.6 XS919 C 11 Squadron at Wattisham on 24 April 1968. This aircraft was first flown on 28 September 1966 and delivered to 11 Squadron on 14 April 1967. It was also operated by 56 Squadron in Cyprus and 5 Squadron at Binbrook. (*Philip Birtles*)

Above: Lightning F.6 XS931 G 11 Squadron on the flight line at Wattisham on 24 April 1968. This aircraft was first flown on 31 March 1967 and was delivered to 11 Squadron on 31 May 1967. It was struck off charge on 25 May 1979. (*Philip Birtles*)

Below: Lightning F.6 XS934 K 11 Squadron at Le Bourget on 5 June 1971, showing a range of external stores, including a large underwing fuel tank. This aircraft was first flown on 11 May 1967 and delivered to 11 Squadron on 3 July 1967. It was delivered to 56 Squadron in Cyprus, but crashed in the sea on 3 April 1973, with the pilot successfully ejecting. (*Philip Birtles*)

Lightning F3/6 XR760 H 23 Squadron landing at Farnborough on 8 September 1970. This aircraft was first flown on 29 September 1965 and was delivered to 5 Squadron on 15 February 1966. After modification to full F.6 standard, it was also operated by 56 Squadron in Cyprus and finally with LTF at Binbrook. (*Philip Birtles*)

At Leuchars, 23 Squadron began replacing its Lightning F.3s with interim F.3/6s in May 1967, but by the end of the year they had all been replaced by full specification F.6s, including XS938, the last one for the RAF. This aircraft was lost on 28 April 1971 when a reheat fire was experienced, and following a successful ejection, it crashed into the River Tay. Two 23 Squadron F.6s, XR725 and XS936 flew non-stop across the Atlantic for the Canadian National Show in Toronto, leaving Leuchars on 28 August and returning on 3 September 1968, after performing there and at other displays.

Lightning F.3/6 XR762 L 23 Squadron at Wattisham on 24 April 1968. This aircraft was first flown on 9 October 1965 and delivered to 5 Squadron on 22 February 1966. Following modification to F.6 configuration, it was delivered to 23 Squadron on 29 December 1967 and was operated by 11 Squadron from December 1973. (*Philip Birtles*)

Above: Lightning F.6 XS937 C 23 Squadron carrying Skyflash on the flight line at Wattisham on 24 April 1968. This aircraft was first flown on 26 June 1967 and delivered to 23 Squadron on 21 August 1967. (*Philip Birtles*)

Below: Last production Lightning F.6 XS938 E 23 Squadron at Wattisham on 24 April 1968. This aircraft was first flown on 30 June 1967 and was delivered to 23 Squadron on 28 August 1967. It crashed into the River Tay on 28 April 1971 and the pilot ejected safely. (*Philip Birtles*)

23 Squadron Lightning F.6s XR754 M, XR747 K, XS937 C and XR928 D. (*BAE Systems*)

Both 11 and 23 Squadrons were kept busy from Leuchars from 1969 to 1972, intercepting Soviet reconnaissance aircraft mainly around the north of Scotland into the Atlantic but occasionally they flew down the east coast of Britain and were met by Binbrook's QRA Lightnings.

When 56 Squadron deployed to Cyprus in April 1967, 29 Squadron with Javelin FAW.9s at Akrotiri exchanged places and re-equipped with Lightning F.3s at Wattisham on 1 May as the last RAF Lightning unit. The first aircraft to be delivered was T.5 XS422 on 10 May, followed by ex-23 and 74 Squadron F.3s which it retained until December 1974; 29 Squadron never flying F.6s, but converting to Phantoms. The maximum Lightning strength with the RAF was in 1972, when eight squadrons flew Lightnings, five of which were responsible for the defence of UK airspace. To provide round the clock coverage, each squadron was split into two flights, one responsible for day and the other night flying, and continued in the Lightning force until they were finally retired. Training continued in practice interceptions, continuation flying, in-flight refuelling and short overseas deployments. In addition, each Lightning squadron was deployed to the Missile Practice Camp (MPC) at Valley to allow air-to-air missile practice over the Cardigan Bay ranges, usually with Firestreak acquisition rounds against a heat source towed behind a pilotless Jindivik drone.

Above: Lightning F.6 XR773 N 56 Squadron at Leconfield on 18 July 1973 with overwing fuel tanks. This aircraft was first flown on 28 February 1966 and was delivered to 74 Squadron on 7 November 1966. It then passed to 56 Squadron in Cyprus. (*Adrian Balch collection*)

Below: Lightning F.6 XS897 S 56 Squadron at Lakenheath 2 August 1975. This aircraft was first flown on 10 May 1966 and delivered to 74 Squadron on 21 December 1966. It passed to 56 Squadron in Cyprus and crashed 26 May 1970. (*John Hughes via Adrian Balch collection*)

Lightning F.6 XS933 K 56 Squadron at Coningsby 29 May 1975. This aircraft was first flown on 27 April 1967 and was delivered to 11 Squadron on 23 June 1967, after which it went to 56 Squadron in Cyprus. (*Adrian Balch collection*)

From 1971, RAF Lightning F.6s finally gained twin Aden 30mm cannon gun armament which had been developed for the export versions, fitted in the forward section of the ventral fuel tank. It was no longer impotent after firing the missiles and could be used in a secondary air-to-ground role. In July 1974, 56 Squadron found itself in the midst of a delicate situation when the Cyprus National Guard staged a coup against President Archbishop Makarios. An emergency was declared from 20 to 27 July and the Lightnings were brought to instant readiness, with Turkish aerial activity increasing. Over 200 sorties were flown by 56 Squadron, avoiding any potential situations during a very tense period with a high level of aircraft availability. It provided good experience, not just for the pilots, but also for ground crew and operations personnel.

Akrotiri was then one of the RAF's major bases, but in the defence review of 1975, the station had all the operational squadrons removed and was left with a single search and rescue unit. However, it was soon realised that Akrotiri was an ideal site for Armament Practice Camps (APC), which was used by many active RAF squadrons for weapons and tactical training. Pilots were able to engage in air-to-air gunnery training which cannot be simulated, like missile firing. To deploy to Cyprus, the Lightnings needed six in-flight refuelling for the F.6s, and ten for the shorter endurance T.5s. Often F.3s were in the deployments to provide high-speed targets, while live firing was against targets towed by Canberras. It was normal for Lightning squadrons to spend five weeks in Cyprus to achieve their required NATO qualifications. Each squadron was split into two flights, alternating between live firing training and operational awareness. Before firing live ammunition at the towed target, pilots first had to prove they were safe by making cine film attacks. Akrotiri is now one of the busiest RAF stations, responding to the many tensions in the Middle East.

The Watttisham Wing was the first station to relinquish its Lightnings, with 111 Squadron disbanding on 30 September 1974 after only four months with F.6s, followed by F.3 equipped 29 Squadron on 31 December. No. 56 Squadron returned from Cyprus to Wattisham on 21 January 1975 and disbanded on 28 June 1976. Meanwhile, 23 Squadron with F.6s disbanded at Leuchars on 31 October 1975.

Above: Lightning F.6 XR747 X 111 Squadron on approach to Wattisham in August 1974. This aircraft was first flown on 2 April 1965 and was delivered to 23 Squadron on 4 January 1968 before briefly operated by 111 Squadron. (A*drian Balch collection*)

Below: Lightning F.6 XR752 Y 111 Squadron take off from Wattisham. This aircraft was first flown on 20 April 1964 and delivered to 74 Squadron on 1 June 1964. It passed to 111 Squadron when it suffered Cat.5 damage in a mid-air collision with a Mirage III on 20 May 1971. It landed safely and was used for spares as 8166M. (*Garry Lakin collection*)

7

Binbrook Lightnings

The final Lightning units were 5 and 11 Squadrons at Binbrook with C Flight 11 Squadron responsible for conversion training. The training was formalised in October 1975 by the formation of the Lightning Training Flight (LTF) with all Binbrook based units operating F.3s, F.6s and T.5s. As part of 11 Group, RAF Strike Command, the Binbrook squadrons played a major part in the air defence of the UK and had been a Lightning station since 1965 when 5 Squadron had reformed and was joined by 11 Squadron in 1972. As well as the LTF providing conversion training, there was also the Lightning Augmentation Force (LAF) which supplied additional reserve operational aircraft during exercises and in times of increased tension.

Lightning F.6 XS925 L 5 Squadron in metal finish at Binbrook armed with Firestreak drill rounds and with ventral cannon pack. This aircraft first flew from Samlesbury on 26 January 1967 and was delivered to 5 Squadron on 2 March 1967. It was also operated by 11 Squadron, latterly from 14 June 1985, and is now preserved at the RAF Museum, Hendon. (*Philip Birtles*)

Above: Lightning F.6 XS919 F 5 Squadron in top-side camouflage with ventral Aden gun pack at Abingdon on 16 September 1978. This aircraft was first flown on 28 September 1966 and was delivered to 11 Squadron on 14 April 1967. It served with 56 Squadron in Cyprus and was then delivered to 5 Squadron. (*Philip Birtles*)

Below: Lightning F.6 XS901 A 5 Squadron with Red Top drill round and ventral gun pack at Finningley on 29 July 1977. First flown on 1 July 1966, this aircraft was delivered to 5 Squadron, followed by 56 Squadron, before going to 11 Squadron. (*Philip Birtles*)

Above: Lightning F.6 XS928 AH 5 Squadron in two-tone grey camouflage finish at Mildenhall. This aircraft was first flown on 28 February 1967 and was delivered to 11 Squadron on 4 April 1967. It served with 74 Squadron in Singapore, then 23, 56 and 11 Squadrons before joining 5 Squadron. (*Garry Lakin*)

Below: Lightning F.3 XR770 AA 5 Squadron in special light grey colour scheme at Binbrook. This aircraft first flew on 16 December 1966 and was delivered to 74 Squadron on 26 September 1966. Before delivery, it appeared at the Farnborough Air Show in September 1966 wearing Saudi Arabian markings. (*Garry Lakin*)

Above: A trio of 5 Squadron Lightning F6s: XS899 AF, XS932 AG and XS936 AB in a selection of overall grey finishes. (*BAE Systems*)

Below: Lightning F.6 XS928 D 11 Squadron in natural metal finish at Benson on 20 September 1969. (*Philip Birtles*)

Above: Lightning F.6 XS931 G 11 Squadron fitted with overwing fuel tanks at Abingdon on 14 June 1968. This aircraft was delivered to 11 Squadron on 31 May 1967 and was struck off charge on 25 May 1979. (*Philip Birtles*)

Below: Lightning F.6 XR773 D 11 Squadron with squadron markings on fin and armed with Red Top and ventral cannons. This aircraft was first flown on 28 February 1966 and delivered to 74 Squadron on 7 November 1966. It was passed on to 56 Squadron in Cyprus, and then returned to Britain where it joined 11 Squadron. (*Philip Birtles*)

Above: Lightning F.3 XR720 M 11 Squadron armed with Red Top, but no ventral gun pack in camouflage finish at Greenham Common on 31 July 1976. This aircraft was first flown on 24 December 1964 and was delivered to 33 MU at Lyneham on 29 March 1965. It was delivered to 11 Squadron in December 1973 and passed to the LTF in 1983. (*Philip Birtles*)

Below: Lightning F.6 XR724 11 Squadron with top-side camouflage finish, armed with Red Top and fitted with ventral gun pack. This aircraft was first flown on 10 February 1965 as an F.3 and converted to F.6 before delivery to 11 Squadron on 16 June 1967. It was withdrawn from use at Binbrook by 1983. (*Philip Birtles collection*)

Above: Lightning F.3/6 XR759 BJ 11 Squadron in two-tone grey camouflage finish armed with Red Top and ventral gun pack. This aircraft was first flown on 9 September 1965 and delivered to 5 Squadron on 18 January 1966. It was fully modified as an F.6, delivered to 60 MU on 2 August 1968 and issued to 56 Squadron. By 1983, it was with 11 Squadron at Binbrook. (*Garry Lakin*)

Below: Lightning F.3/6 XR754 BC 11 Squadron and carrying the name Flt Lt Ian Black, the last RAF pilot to qualify on the Lightning, at Mildenhall 28 May 1988. It is armed with Red Top and the 30mm Aden ventral gun pack. This aircraft was first flown on 8 July 1965 and was delivered to A&AEE Boscombe Down on 3 December 1965. It was issued to the AFDS in March 1966 and then modified to full F.6 standard at Warton from 31 January 1967. It was then operated by 23, 5 and 11 Squadrons. (*Garry Lakin*)

Lightning F.3/6 XR759 11 Squadron in overall light grey camouflage and fitted with overwing fuel tanks. It is armed with Red Top and fitted with the ventral gun pack, at Brize Norton on 11 June 1983. (*Philip Birtles*)

With the reduced requirement for pilot training, 226 OCU at Coltishall closed. The initial plan for C Flight 11 Squadron was unworkable—an operational squadron was unable to support a conversion training role as well. The LTF was therefore formed to provide sufficient numbers of pilots to support the Lightning force until its planned retirement in 1988. With all Lightning operations concentrated at Binbrook, there were over eighty aircraft on the station consisting of some F.1A non-airworthy decoys, an abandoned T.4 and a large stock of F.3s, T.5s and F.6s. With plentiful stock of airworthy F.3s, there were still enough for 5 and 11 Squadrons to practice combat and aerobatic training on an aircraft lighter than the combat ready F.6s. There were also adequate aircraft available for the LTF which had eight aircraft consisting of four each: F.3s and T.5s with a large stock of replacements in storage. Now a self-contained unit, the LTF moved into the centre 'C' Type hangar behind the air traffic control tower. By 1978, an F.6 was allocated to the LTF as a high fatigue life target for air-to-air weapons training. This aircraft, always flown by a staff pilot, had a forward 75-gallon fuel tank replacing the Aden guns. A Luneberg lens was fitted in the nose to help students identify the aircraft.

One of the early LTF tasks was to develop a suitable camouflage for the entire Lightning fleet using the grounded decoys on the airfield, but nothing conclusive resulted. Various combinations of grey and green were tested until a pair of T.5s were painted, one in grey and the other in NATO green. The result was a compromise with the entire fleet painted in grey and green, which proved effective for low level operations over land and sea, but not at altitude. In future years, various tones of grey were adopted making the aircraft even less conspicuous with toned down national markings, a great contrast from the creative styles used in the 1960s.

Trainee pilots posted to the LTF would have completed their basic flying training on Jet Provosts, followed by advanced training on Hawks at Valley, by which time

Above: Lightning F.3 XP751 LTF in natural metal finish. This aircraft was first flown on 16 March 1964 and delivered to 74 Squadron as first fully operational F.3. It also served with 111, 29 and 5 Squadrons before issue to LTF. (*Garry Lakin*)

Below: Lightning F.3 XP750 with LTF in standard camouflage upper surfaces on approach to Binbrook. This aircraft was first flown on 3 January 1964 and was delivered to the CFE. It was modified to F.6 standard and issued to 111 Squadron in 1972 (*Garry Lakin*)

they would have earned their wings. This was followed by combat training with the Tactical Weapons Unit (TWU) at Brawdy for those selected for fast jet operations. The choices of aircraft types were quite varied compared with the modern RAF, with pilots selected for single-seat or multi-crew duties. For ground attack, the single-seat choice was between Harrier or Jaguar and Tornado GR.1 and Buccaneer with pilot and navigator/weapons operators. For air defence, the choice was between the two crew Phantom FG.1/FGR.2 or the single-seat Lightning. Although it was from an earlier era, only the best TWU graduates were posted on to the Lightning. This was due to the

Above: LTF Lightning F3 XP753 in two-tone grey camouflage at Binbrook with the name Flt Lt Thompson below the cockpit. This aircraft was first flown on 8 May 1964 and was issued to 74 Squadron on 23 June 1964. It served with 29 Squadron in 1972 and the following year, went to 11 Squadron. When with the LTF, it crashed off Scarborough on 26 August 1983 with the loss of the pilot. (*Garry Lakin*)

Below: Lightning F.6 XS936 DF LTF with upper surfaces camouflaged at Mildenhall carrying the name Wg Cdr D E North below the cockpit. This aircraft was first flown on 31 May 1967 and went to 60 MU on 27 July 1967 before issue to 23 Squadron on 23 August 1967. It went to 11 Squadron on 2 June 1976. (*Garry Lakin*)

exceptionally high cockpit workload where the pilot was responsible for the complete weapons system operation without the more modern aids. The novice pilot had to be able to master tracking a gyrating target Hawk, leading to the air combat phase where good scores had to be achieved. In addition, there had to be a high level of proficiency in instrument flying and low-level simulated attack, demonstrating an ability to cope in an unpredictable high workload situation.

Following successful selection from the TWU to fly Lightnings, the next stage was the Aviation Medical Department at North Luffenham where the candidate was checked for fit into the snug cockpit while wearing the protective survival clothing, including an immersion suit. A thorough medical check was made to check suitability for sustained high altitude operations, all before travelling to Binbrook to join the LTF, where all the instructors had completed at least one Lightning tour. All the staff pilots were either Qualified Flying Instructors (QFIs), Intercept Weapons Instructors (IWIs) or Tactical Instructors (TIs) and the course began with two-week ground school lectures to understand the aircraft systems covering airframe, engines, electrics, hydraulics and fuel management. Radar and weapons systems were covered later when flying training had started. During the second week, emergency drills and handling exercises were covered in the simulator.

The new pilot was then ready to start the demanding Conversion Exercises (CONVEX) stage of the programme, which normally consisted of five initial dual sorties in a T.5, followed by the first solo. Training then continued, expanding the handling capabilities in a mixture of dual and solo sorties starting with ten circuits and approaches, although touch and goes were never flown in the Lightning due to heavy wear on tyres and brakes. The next phase of training was instrument flying, assisted by the simulator resulting in passing the Instrument Rating Test (IRT) which could take as long as two weeks. Then, in contrast, pilots would become familiar with close and tactical formation flying, culminating in a handling check flight, ready for the radar handling phase.

As with all aircraft, before flying, it was essential to complete a walk-round visual inspection by the pilot, and the Lightning was no exception, going around from the nose on the right hand (starboard) side in a clockwise circuit. On approaching, the chocks are checked in place, and a fire extinguisher was available. While moving around the aircraft, ground crew removed any intake blanks, pitot covers and undercarriage locks. The Lightning engine intake with radar fairing were checked for any damage, before moving down the starboard side of the fuselage under the wing checking for any damage and fuel leaks from unapproved areas. Tyres and brakes were carefully inspected, as they suffered high loads and had a limited life. If one was worn or damaged, it could be changed in a few minutes by ground engineers. Accumulator gauges had to be checked to have readings within limits. The tailpipe required inspection for any molten metal lumps which could be the sign of a pending failure, and the cable for the brake parachute also checked for any damage. On the left (port) side rear, the fire extinguisher contents had to be checked and on the way to the cockpit access ladder, the weapons pack was inspected. Once at the top of the ladder, an inspection was made of the upper wing surfaces to check for fuel venting.

Now in the snug cockpit, the pilot made sure the ejection seat pins were stowed, closed the canopy and started his checks, scanning the switches, instruments and controls ready to signal the engine start sequence and removal of the chocks ready to taxi under instructions from air traffic ready to blast off on another sortie.

After the first LTF sortie, when the student demonstrated his ability to make a safe landing, the second flight was a demonstration of aerobatics, which, due to the high fuel consumption was only for 20–25 minutes with an instrument approach and landing at the end. The other three dual sorties usually consisted of more circuit flying or covering any weak areas and a practice emergency diversion to another airfield. Before being cleared to fly solo, the trainee had to experience a simulator check giving experience of many potential emergencies. Following a final sortie in a T.5, the pilot was cleared for his first solo in a F.3 with full responsibility for the safe operation of the aircraft, before making a landing and taxiing back to the Binbrook flight line.

Having learned to fly the Lightning, the next stage was to learn how to operate the aircraft as a weapon system. The first solo was followed by two dual sorties to cover supersonic handling and demanding high rate turns, followed by the instrument flying phase, culminating in a preliminary instrument rating. Battle formation flying at low level and tail chases had to be mastered using hand signals to maintain radio silence. For this exercise, the aircraft usually operated in pairs. Once these exercises had been completed, a mid-course handling check was made to assess the student's progress after flying 25 to 30 hours on the type and included an unplanned simulated emergency diversion.

The student was then back to ground school to learn about the radar operation and the associated Firestreak and Red Top missiles, with exercises practiced on the simulator, before being used in practice. It would take up to six months of practice to become familiar with the radar operation in all weathers and attitudes. In addition, the pilot needed to manage the weapons systems and identify the target in poor visibility, while ensuring enough fuel remained to complete the tasks. This was a

Lightning F.6 XS936 DF LTF in overall light grey camouflage at Abingdon on 18 September 1982. This aircraft was also operated by 5 Squadron from 30 May 1985 and last flew on 24 November 1987. It is now displayed with Castle Air in Cornwall. (*Philip Birtles*)

Above: Lightning F.6 XR773 with Binbrook Station Flight in camouflage upper surfaces carrying Red Top and with ventral gun pack, at Waddington on 29 May 1981. This aircraft first flew on 28 February 1966 and was delivered to 74 Squadron on 7 November 1966, followed by 56 Squadron in Cyprus. (*Philip Birtles*)

Below: Lightning T.5 XS458 DY LTF in camouflage finish at Mildenhall on 28 May 1988. This aircraft was first flown on 3 December 1966 and was delivered to 226 OCU at Coltishall on 2 February 1966. It was delivered to 11 Squadron before going to LTF. (*Garry Lakin*)

Above: First production Lightning T.5 XS416 V LTF in camouflage finish at Greenham Common on 30 May 1980. It was first flown on 20 August 1964 and delivered to 226 OCU on 16 July 1965. It was operated by 11 Squadron before joining the LTF. (*Philip Birtles*)

Below: Lightning T.5 XS458 LTF in mid-grey camouflage on approach to Binbrook. This aircraft was first flown on 3 December 1966 and delivered to 226 OCU on 2 February 1966. It was with 11 Squadron in 1983 (*Garry Lakin*)

time so demanding that some pilots were unable to fly the Lightning and interpret the radar due to the high workload, resulting in the student being suspended from training. Only the highest standards could be tolerated to cope with the demands of the aircraft.

When compared with more modern replacements, the Lightning was limited by its short endurance, with an average unrefueled sortie time of 55 minutes. Flight refuelling was often used to extend the duration, but time on station was limited by pilot fatigue with restrictions in the tight cockpit with an anti-g suit, survival gear including an immersion suit and breathing oxygen continuously, all of which challenges the pilot's concentration. The Binbrook Lightnings had the responsibility for the defence of the UK in times of high threat and monitoring UK airspace in peacetime. The QRA pilots needed to identify targets, day and night in all weathers, 365 days of the year. It also had responsibility for defence of the Royal Navy at sea within NATO waters and made occasional overseas deployment.

With its short endurance, Lightning operations almost always relied on in-flight refuelling. Lightnings were therefore fitted with flight refuelling probe under the port wing leading edge. As already mentioned, 56 Squadron were responsible for initial flight refuelling trials in July 1962, when, after training and assessment they were refuelled by Valiant tankers during a deployment to Cyprus. To investigate interoperability with the Fleet Air Arm, 111 Squadron operated with Sea Vixens carrying 'buddy' refuelling pods. With the early retirement of Valiants, 19 Squadron undertook trials with the replacement Victor K.1 in 1965. While Victor tankers were being urgently converted to fill the gap in air-to-air refuelling capacity, USAF KC-135 tankers fitted with underwing refuelling pods undertook trials with 23 Squadron also in 1965.

The tankers routinely patrolled at predetermined points along a planned deployment route, or on patrol over the North Sea to assist in training exercises and QRA operations. The tanker normally flew at 300mph along a 'race-track' pattern ready for the Lightnings to arrive. The fighter pilots normally operated in pairs, approaching from the port side from where they were called in by the tanker crew. If there were two Lightnings, the first would go below the tanker tail and link up with the trailing starboard hose and drogue, while the second joined with the port installation. Within 2 minutes, 300 gallons (1,363 litres) of fuel was transferred, and the Lightning eased back and moved over to the starboard side to make room for the next aircraft.

Great care had to be taken to make a slow approach to plugging in the probe. The correct way was to follow the indicators on the tanker to align the probe with the drogue and not try to follow the often-wavering drogue. There were signal lights under the tanker rear to allow both day and night refuelling. With a red light showing, the tanker was not ready, but with an amber light, the Lightning could move up and make contact. The approach was made at plus 3 to 5 knots, or a fast-walking speed to contact with the probe, which then slowly wound in until a good contact was made, opening the tanker fuel valves. Then the green light would come on and fuel flow commenced. If there were two aircraft being refuelled, they would wait until both had full tanks, at which point they would both disconnect and break to starboard to clear the tanker.

Using the signal lights sequence allowed not only night operations, but also for reasons for radio silence or communications failure. The pilot requiring fuel transfer attracted the tanker crew attention by flying along the port side. Once seen by the tanker crew, the hoses were trailed and the fighter pilot moved around to the rear to take on fuel.

In the deployment of 11 Squadron with Lightning F.6s to Asia, flight refuelling was used on much of the 18,500 miles from RAF Victor K.2 tankers of 55, 57 and 214 Squadrons. Leaving Leuchars on 6 January 1967, the first leg was 4,000 miles to Bahrain where the Lightnings landed. The next stop was at Gan in the Indian Ocean and Singapore was reached after just two days, proving the capability of rapid deployment in times of tension. During the out and back flights, over 228 refuelling contacts were made, demonstrating how important flight refuelling capability was to combat operations.

Binbrook became the major Lightning engineering base including major overhauls and modifications, and QRA readiness was maintained. There were a number of exchange visits to and from NATO bases in Europe, and the threat had changed from high level to below the radar, where the Lightning was even more range restricted, but was still an effective defence. It was not only potential hostile reconnaissance aircraft which required investigation, but also sometimes an aircraft lost and without communications, which needed direction to a safe landing.

The 25th anniversary of the Lightning entering service with the RAF was celebrated on 3 August 1979 at Binbrook. One of the highlights was a line-up of eight specially-marked Lightnings representing 19, 23, 56, 74, 92 and 111 Squadrons, in addition to the two resident units.

With the Lightnings continuing to serve into the 1980s, the Southern QRA was shared between Binbrook, Wattisham and Coningsby, with Binbrook responsible for two weeks in every five. Two Lightnings were on the alert in the Q-shed armed with live missiles, loaded cannons and fully fuelled, ready to go at a moment's notice. When an alert was raised, one Lightning was scrambled, with the second ready to go if the first went unserviceable. The Lightnings would often intercept and shadow Russian surveillance aircraft, which could be Tu-95 Bears, Tu-16 Badgers, M-4 Bisons or Il-18 Coots. These aircraft usually routed around the North Cape towards Britain and out into the Atlantic.

Although the QRA Lightnings were armed with Red Top missiles, the main weapon of choice was the 30mm cannons fitted in the forward part of the ventral fuel tank. This allowed a warning shot to catch the attention of more stubborn potential hostile aircraft, without shooting them down. As QRA was the main role of the Binbrook Lightnings, all new pilots were trained for this role. This training involved multiple practice intercepts against any airborne threat, reaching a basic phase which qualified them for QRA duties as limited operational.

With the entire Lightning fleet based at Binbrook, the full range of engineering and maintenance was concentrated in one place, which was a unique situation at the time. First line maintenance consisted of daily checks, with topping up of fluids such as fuel, oil and hydraulic fluid, correcting any simple snags to keep the aircraft available on the flight line and ready for operations. Second line maintenance involved major scheduled servicing, plus any repairs and modifications which could ground the aircraft for a number of weeks. Third line servicing would normally be undertaken at a specialist maintenance unit and involved significant disassembly, major repairs and if necessary, preparation for storage. Fourth line maintenance would usually involve work by the manufacturer at the original production line incorporating major modification programmes and repairs beyond the scope of MUs, but in the case of the Lightning, all engineering was based at Binbrook.

With an aircraft as complex and advanced as the Lightning, first line maintenance often included preventive actions by the highly experienced team of engineers in an airframe and engines with restricted access. The more sophisticated the systems, the more there was to go wrong. This maintenance consisted of pre-flight checks, turnaround between flights and post flight, when fuel, oil, hydraulics and oxygen would be checked. With the high-pressure tyres and landing loads, tyre wear needed constant checking, the break parachute needed replacing, and the external airframe needed checking for any damage. In addition, any minor faults required correcting, allowing the aircraft to be declared ready for its next sortie. The second line maintenance was planned to a schedule depending upon the number of hours flown. A check 1 was carried out every 75 flying hours and took about two days to complete. It consisted of an airframe wash plus greasing and lubrication of certain parts, which were closely inspected. The use of non-destructive testing (NDT) was used to check for any structural fatigue cracking, and as a result of the earlier internal fires, the fuel and hydraulic pipes in the hot zones were carefully checked for any leaks and overall integrity.

A check 2 was carried out every 225 hours and was the first in-depth inspection, including opening up the many panels giving access to the engines and systems for detailed checking. While the main object was to look for faults, wear, corrosion and distortions experienced during the previous 225 hours were checked and random rectifications were also embodied.

Check 3s were carried out by the Aircraft Servicing Flight every 450 hours, which was a second line servicing complex within the Engineering Wing. The main purpose was to continue to inspect for any deterioration and check the integrity of the airframe and systems. This usually required component removal and bench checked for performance. Any non-urgent deferred defects were corrected during this major service.

The biggest item was the 900-hour major check which repeated the check 3; the aircraft was stripped down to its basic structure with a thorough NDT check to for any major deterioration, and appropriate repairs made. This stage could also involve the incorporation of major modifications, involving manufacturer's working parties, when a specialist production line could be set up in a dedicated hangar. The aircraft were sometimes repainted, and the weight and balance limits checked after this service. Not all inspections were based on flying hours, as some could be on-condition, where regular visual checks were required. Out-of-phase servicing included ejection seats, which were inspected every six months, brakes every seventy landings and undercarriage retraction inspected every 100 retractions.

Even this formal programme of inspection did not cover everything; random items between major checks failed due to normal use and were replaced as required. In addition to the airframe and engines, many of the systems had failures, including radar, automatic pilot and weapons—failure of which was not catastrophic, but reduced the effectiveness of the aircraft.

A modern combat aircraft was a large collection of modifications, all stemming from the original general arrangement (GA) drawing. At some point, the level of design reached the stage when initial production was able to start, but the manufacturer's design team would continue to make improvements, initially as a result of early flight development. As the aircraft entered service, further improvements were made to improve safety, performance, effectiveness and increase airframe life. The Lightning was originally designed as a Mach 2 experimental aircraft but it gradually evolved into a potent all-weather interceptor with secondary ground attack capability. The Lightning maintenance engineers were often faced with having to remove a tightly fitting engine just to get access to vital components. Access panels were often small and infrequent when trying to access parts, requiring a high level of dedication by the ground crew.

The major parameter in declaring the service life of the Lightnings was metal fatigue in primary structure, which determined the eventual out-of- service life of the type. The aircraft, by their very nature, were flown aggressively. In order to determine a safe life, a complete aircraft was dynamically tested in a ground rig, simulating typical operational loads anticipated during its operational life. A benefit of this ground testing could result in an extended service life, while the test aircraft was always well ahead of the in-service fleet. Some sorties were more aggressive than others and had to be taken into consideration when the aircraft was flown. To measure the stresses in the flying aircraft, they were fitted with fatigue meters, which was an accelerometer which kept a record of the airframe loads and stresses. When in active combat flying at low level and high-speed training in high manoeuvres, it could consume fatigue life at up to six times the average rate, much of which could not be reproduced in the test rig. High-speed, low-level flying probably used up ten times more fatigue life than a medium to high altitude transit flight. Increased weight contributed heavily to fatigue, and landings also provide additional loads, particularly on the undercarriage.

The recording of fatigue can only be measured as vertical G on the aircraft centre of gravity, and was dependent upon aircraft weight, and stores configuration. Some of the aircraft structure could not be measured by the fatigue meter. Some examples include outer wings, tail assembly and control surfaces; this required the structural designer to make estimates based on experience and the type of sorties flown.

Following the demanding six-month LTF course, pilots were then allocated to a front line work-up to eventually achieve operational status. With the declaration of Limited Operational, pilots could be allocated to QRA duties and participate on any regular sorties with the limitation of only leading two aircraft. When on QRA duties, the aircraft and pilot were at 10 minutes readiness with everything ready to go around the clock in all weathers. Once cleared to this level, training commenced to fully operational state, when the pilot could lead four or more aircraft and assist in training junior pilots. Once declared fully operational, the pilot was allocated a particular Lightning with his name painted on the port side below the canopy.

By the time Binbrook became the home of the Lightnings, there was a very experienced group of pilots with the squadrons, with one pilot, Squadron Leader Dave Carden achieving over 3,000 hours on Lightnings, two more with over 2,500 and around a dozen with over 2,000 hours. With its notoriously unrefueled short endurance of around one hour, that was a lot of flying. It was not just QRA duties, but it included low level Combat Air Patrol Exercise (CAPEX) often with four Lightnings and full flight refuelling support. The flight refuelling was at an altitude above the low-level operation and time would have to be allowed to refuel all four Lightnings. Typical opposition could be up to ten pairs of ground attack Jaguars against a designated target, with the Jaguars also armed with air-to-air missiles. The CAPEX could approach over the sea with the target located on land, which was a challenge to protect and avoid hitting any ground features with the aircraft. The Lightnings always operated as pairs, covering each other as in all air-to-air combat, with a need to maintain knowledge of fuel state and geographical position.

The aircraft took-off in pairs, initially at 85 per cent power, and after take-off reheat was selected with undercarriage retracted and flaps up. Once established in the climb, reheat was cancelled to conserve fuel and the four Lightnings formed up in a battle formation, which was 3,000 yards between pairs. The formation then headed out at low level to the designated operating area with the pilots checking radar, weapons, systems and fuel state while maintaining the formation. The aircraft reached the Combat Air Patrol (CAP) area and while maintaining radio silence, searched for the approaching Jaguars, with the team split into two, not too distant pairs. The 'hostile' force was sighted and the first 'destroyed' in a surprise attack by the camera gun, but the remainder of the attack force was alerted and it became a dog fight with aircraft in all directions in violent manoeuvres using the cannon camera guns which were most effective in close combat. With four Jaguars claimed, they headed away and it was time for the Lightnings, in groups of four, to take on fuel at 30,000 feet from a waiting tanker, two at a time from the underwing pods. Fuel was transferred at the rate of 1,000lb a minute. While one pair was being refuelled, the other pair provided protective cover in the case of threat. Once all the Lightnings were refuelled, the CAPEX continued with the Lightnings descending back down to low level; this time as a four aircraft flight when another formation of Jaguars were spotted and attacked using camera guns against the aggressors until the exercise is complete. The Lightnings were then, once again, running low on fuel. They landed back at Binbrook after only 1 hour and 15 minutes airborne and taxied to the 5 Squadron dispersal, where the ground crew began the attend to any unserviceabilities and prepared the aircraft for the next sorties.

In addition to the day-to-day ongoing training and QRA duties at Binbrook, the pilots were required to maintain their combat skills in air-to-air gunnery. To achieve this, 5 and 11 Squadrons deployed to an Armament Practice Camp (APC) at Akrotiri in Cyprus, together with half the LTF staff pilots, for all to achieve and maintain currency. In Cyprus, weather conditions were more predictable and there were large areas of uncongested air space available. The squadrons would deploy in turn, sharing air transport and ground equipment over the total deployment period. The 30mm Aden cannon gun pack was located under the fuselage, ahead of the ventral fuel tank, and despite the location, there were never any problems.

In preparation for the APC, any pilots who had not fired the guns in the last year were given a refresher in a T.5 with the squadron weapons officer over the North

Sea prior to departure. Although the T.5 was not equipped with guns, the exercise consisted of cine runs on a towed banner target.

The deployment could be quite challenging with up to ten venerable aircraft flying to Cyprus in one day, not only requiring in-flight refuelling, but also ensuring full serviceability. Early deployments had been staging through France, Italy and Greece, but aircraft in the air were less likely to experience difficulties, resulting in air-to-air tanking becoming the preferred option. A week before the deployment, a crew would fly to Marham to brief on the details including fuel uplift, route and radio procedures, tanking brackets and possible diversions in the event of an emergency. On deployment departure day, the engineers would be up before dawn preparing the Lightnings for an early departure, to achieve a reasonable landing time at Akrotiri, while allowing for the two-hour time difference. When everything was ready, the Lightnings would depart in groups of three or four aircraft with a T.5 at the rear. Should any Lightning need to return, the space would be allocated to aircraft flown by LTF or other squadron pilots as airborne spares, returning to Binbrook after the main force had successfully departed the British coast. Although the T.5 was the most difficult to deploy, due to its shorter endurance requiring up to ten tanker contacts, it was valuable for maintaining pilots' currency for all the regular checks during the six week stay at the APC.

On arrival at Akrotiri, the missiles were unloaded and preparations were made for gun firing. The requirement was for all the pilots to become fully qualified in air-to-air gun firing to fulfil the NATO requirement for air defence pilots. To achieve the required skills, pilots had to place 15 per cent of shots on the flag target twice during a maximum of six sorties. If a pilot failed to achieve this score, he had to start again from the beginning. A scoreboard outside the operations room recorded the individual pilot successes. The targets were towed by Wyton based modified 100 Squadron Canberras, who maintained a long-term detachment in Cyprus for the use of all the RAF air defence squadrons. The towed banner was white, 6-foot by 30-foot woven hessian, towed 300 yards behind the aircraft, which would fly to the live firing range 25 miles off the coast with a maximum speed of 200 knots. Once the Canberra was established on range, the first pair of Lightnings was cleared to start engines—ready to take-off for the exercise. The ideal firing speed was 350 knots and directions were given for the Lightning pilots to steer to find the tug.

Flying as the traditional pair, the lead pilot would set up to attack with the Canberra flying in a figure of eight patterns at 8,000 feet. When the tug was on a steady heading, the lead Lightning would plan to be 2,800 yards behind the banner, ready for the pilot to prepare and select guns, although the initial passes were made with cine to ensure all was safe and ready. Once cleared for live firing with inert rounds, the Lightning pilot approached to an estimated 500 yards, closing to 400 yards at a 16-degree angle off to avoid hitting the Canberra from the rear, followed by the wingman. After six or seven passes, the first pair returned to Akrotiri making way for the next pair. Each Lightning pilot had a debrief on return to base, comprised of analysis of the cine film results before the pilots were allowed to fire live rounds. Once cleared for live firing, the cannon rounds in each Lightning were dipped in a colour for each aircraft, used to maintain a score of hits on the banner which could be inspected on return to base.

During the course of the APC, the scores increased until each pilot had achieved 'Ace' status. when qualified, the pilot moved on to simulated operational firing, where he only had a limited number of shells to fire in a fixed number of passes; this culminated in an operational shoot to achieve one hit on the banner. For this part of the exercise, only forty rounds were loaded, and it was necessary to achieve one hit on the target over two passes. To make this part more demanding, the Lightning and Canberra were flying towards each other, firing just after passing the tug in a turn before acquiring the banner and firing. If there was enough time left and bullets remaining, the two flights would compete on a shoot. Each of the four aircraft would be loaded with 240 rounds in a number of colours to maintain pilot anonymity, with each flight allocated a banner. As a finale, the squadron flew a diamond nine formation before welcoming the next squadron and returning to Binbrook.

In addition to the APCs in Cyprus, squadron pilots had to be able to fire their air-to-air missiles and attended a Missile Practice Camp (MPC) every year, based at RAF Valley for operations over the Cardigan Bay ranges. Normally, five Red Top or Firestreak missiles were allocated, allowing half the squadron pilots to participate. The deployment was usually expected to last up to two weeks, depending on the weather—limitations on the missiles due to infrared seekers meant that they could only be fired clear of cloud. Usually five single-seat Lightnings were taken on the deployment, plus a two-seater for any photo chase requirements. Before departure from Binbrook, the planned missile attack profiles were practiced on the simulator, followed by the same profile in the air, with aircraft taking it in turns to play the role of target. The two-week preparation also included detailed lectures on the weapons systems. Targets were a flare towed by a Jindivik to avoid if possible, destroying the drone and just scoring on the heat source.

In the spring of 1988, preparations were being made for the final retirement of the Lightnings at Binbrook with 5 Squadron having disbanded on 31 December 1987. The surplus aircraft were put into store to support the remaining Lightning operations with 11 Squadron. There was no relaxing for 11 Squadron in the final rundown to retirement with four F.6s and a T.5 sent to Gutersloh for dissimilar air combat training with Harrier GR.3s. On return to Binbrook, because of delays with the Tornado F.3 radar, six Lightning F.6s were refurbished and fitted with overwing tanks. They were based at Warton for operations over the Aberporth Range against a Foxhunter equipped development Tornado and by the end of March, most of the flights were being made by Warton based pilots. On 11 April, 11 Squadron crews prepared for a final air-to-air combat exercise with 74 Squadron Phantoms from Wattisham. Four Lightnings were allocated against the more sophisticated radar-guided weapons systems carried by the two-crew Phantoms. Among the four Lightnings was F.6 XR769 flown by Flight Lieutenant Dick Coleman on exchange from the Royal Australian Air Force, and a flight refuelling was made from a 57 Squadron tanker in preparation for the exercise. Once fuelling was complete, the Lightnings pulled away, ready to simulate combat with the Phantoms. When fully committed to mock interception, there was a Mayday call over the radio and Lightning XR769 was venting white vapour from the jet pipe. The emergency services were instantly alerted, and on inspection, there was a fire down the left side of the fuselage, creating serious damage. All thought of a traditional return and landing at Binbrook was abandoned and preparations were made to eject over the North Sea with fuel state declining rapidly. The final ejection was made in controlled conditions at 300 knots and 10,000 feet, the pilot landed safely in the sea and climbed into his dinghy. He was soon picked up by a rescue Wessex and returned to Binbrook shortly after the other three aircraft returned. This Lightning was the 74th and last to be lost during 34 years of RAF front line service.

With the final retirement day fast approaching, 11 Squadron put up a diamond nine formation flypast on 29 April 1988 and a final deployment in May when two F.6s and two T.5s attended an affiliation exercise with 12 Squadron Buccaneers from Lossiemouth. With official disbandment on 1 May, the squadron had two months to close down, deliver some aircraft to new homes and close the station. The furthest delivery was F.6 XS929 to Akrotiri as gate guardian in 56 Squadron colours as it once served with the Squadron in Cyprus. The last two F.6s left for Cranfield at the end of June, with the intention to fly them on the civil register, but when this failed, they were scrapped in December 1994, together with other Lightnings, just leaving T.5 XS458 maintained in ground running condition in 11 Squadron markings.

Even after retirement from combat duties with the RAF, there were still flying tasks required as a high-speed target for the development of the Foxhunter radar in its replacement, the Tornado ADV (Air Defence Variant). There were considerable development problems with the radar in this long-range air defence two-crew fighter, which was armed with radar-guided air defence beyond visual range (BVR) Skyflash air-to-air missiles. The development delays were so bad that the initial Tornado F.2 had the radar replaced by concrete ballast, known as the Blue Circle radar. The sole weapons available were two Sidewinder short range air-to-air dog-fight missiles, for which the Tornado was unsuitable.

The MOD Lightning airworthiness certification was extended to allow the aircraft to be operated from Warton on trials. One of these Lightnings in bare metal finish, was XP693, which was built as an F.3 but converted as a hybrid F.6 and had always been used for development flying at Boscombe Down and Warton. Two more ex-5 Squadron Lightning F.6s were identified: XR773 in overall mid-grey and XS904 in camouflage colours. F.6 XR773 was used as a spare and ferried to Boscombe Down for flyable storage if required. F.6 XS928 was also modified, but withdrawn when it was found to have a large structural crack in the airframe and was replaced by XR773 from storage.

To maintain a greater endurance, all three were fitted with overwing tanks which could not be jettisoned. In addition to the Lightnings, Buccaneer S.2 XN974 was also in the Warton test fleet, which was fitted with a flight refuelling pod on the starboard wing to keep the Lightnings in the air longer to cover more complex Tornado development flying.

During the early part of the trials, when Lightnings were still operational with the RAF, service pilots were used on simulated targets because they were more familiar with air defence combat flying than the regular civilian test pilots at Warton. Following the retirement of the type from RAF service and the service pilots posted on to new aircraft, one RAF pilot elected to transfer to Warton, and several new pilots converted without the use of a simulator or T.5 trainer.

The three Lightning F.6s operated by BAe on Foxhunter radar trials for the Tornado F.3 programme. They are XR773 in grey finish, XS904 in camouflage finish and XP693 in natural metal finish. All three were fitted with overwing fuel tanks and the ventral gun packs were replaced by additional fuel tank capacity. (*BAE Systems*)

The trials were over the Cardigan Bay ranges and normally involved complex sorties, with up to three Lightnings against a single development Tornado. With the successful development of the Foxhunter radar in the Tornado F.3, Lightning operations wound down at Warton and the last flight of three Lightnings in formation was on 16 December 1992. The last Lightning flight from Warton was by BAe test pilot Keith Hartley in XP693 on 23 December 1992 when it was flown to Exeter with XR773 to join Barry Pover's Classic Jet Aircraft Company with plans to fly them in Britain. These plans did not materialise and both Lightnings were shipped to Thunder City in Cape Town, where they flew for some years. The last Lightning to fly in the UK was XS904, which joined XR728 at Bruntingthorpe on 21 January 1993, where both aircraft are maintained in running condition in an ORP shed.

8

Lightning Exports

The Lightning should have been a greater success in the export market, but international politics favoured the less practical F-104 in Europe for NATO air forces, even though the type was barely adopted by the USAF. What modest exports that were achieved with Lightnings resulted in significant improvements, which also benefited the RAF with the F.6s. Greater overseas sales would have resulted in an even more practical and effective combat aircraft, removing the many restrictions experienced from its experimental heritage. Lightning development was also restricted from the start following the 1957 Defence White Paper, which affected the entire British aircraft industry's capability.

However, once the early Lightnings were established in RAF service, BAC began to investigate improvements which would make the aircraft attractive to overseas air forces. The first priority was to increase endurance, but also to make it more attractive with roles in addition to pure interception to be developed. The government authorised BAC to improve the range of the aircraft to make it more suitable for overseas deployments, and although the European market was saturated by American designs, there were still good prospects in the Middle East. In Saudi Arabia, the new air force was looking for modern equipment in the early 1960s, a little over a decade since its formation. In 1962, fighting broke out on the Saudi-Yemen border. The Yemen revolutionary forces armed with Russian Mig-17s and Il-28 by the President Nasser, led Egyptian government, which were able to fly over Saudi Arabia without any challenge. The Saudi government therefore decided to acquire a completely new air defence system. With increasing tension and attacks on Saudi towns and settlements in the southeast of the country, Saudi defences were strengthened at the airfield of Kharmis Mushayt, located only 54 miles from the North Yemen border.

While a complete air defence package was being negotiated, an interim deal provided for six Lightnings, six Hunters and a battery of Thunderbird SAMs supplied in a programme known as 'Magic Carpet', which also included pilots, support engineering personnel, air traffic controllers and radar operators. The first four Lightnings were ex-RAF F.2s, redesignated F.52s with the first aircraft, XN796/52-657 departing Britain on 8 July 1966, flown by Tim Ferguson, followed three days later by XN770/52-656 flown by Don Knight. The second pair of F.52s departed for Saudi Arabia on 22 July, and the last two aircraft were T.4s, redesignated T.54s XM989/54-650 and XM992/54-651 which left on 6 June 1966. On arrival, the aircraft were demonstrated to the Saudi population to boost morale, replacing the antiquated F.86 Sabres and B-26 Invaders, but two Lightnings were later lost due to accidents caused by pilot inexperience.

Deployment began to Khamis on 7 August 1967 with an F.52 and T.54 arriving from Riyadh, allowing the Lightnings to be declared fully operational on 13 November. This acted as an effective deterrent, with all incursions by the Egyptian aircraft ceasing. There were difficulties with shortage of spares, and a lack of urgency to scramble when there was an enemy incursion, which frustrated the pilots, since the intruders were back across the border before any order to attack came.

Above: Royal Saudi Air Force Lightning F.52s on the flight line at Warton, converted from ex RAF F.2s. Heading the line is 52-657, which was XN796 with the RAF, but crashed on take-off at Riyadh on 20 September 1966, and was replaced by XN729. (*BAE Systems*)

Below: Lightning T.54 54-651, ex-RAF XM992 at Warton was delivered to Saudi Arabia on 6 June 1966 and served with 6 Squadron. It was first flown on 13 December 1961 and delivered to 111 Squadron on 24 September 1962, and bought by BAC on 7 April 1966. (*BAE Systems*)

Lightning T.54 54-651 taking on fuel from Victor B(K)1 XH620 on its delivery flight to Saudi Arabia. (*BAE Systems*)

Meanwhile, the main export order was confirmed in the House of Commons in December 1965 as one of the largest defence packages achieved by Britain with a total of thrity-four Lightning T.53s based on the F.3, but with many of the improvements of the F.6 plus six T.55s. Also included in the order were twenty-five Strikemasters. The prototype was originally XR722, which left for Saudi Arabia on 28 June 1969, becoming 53-666. Additional armament for ground attack duties included underwing pylons capable of carrying two 1,000lb bombs or two packs of 18-inch 68mm SNEB rocket packs. In addition, a forty-eight 2-inch rocket pack could be carried under the fuselage in retractable units, replacing the air-to-air missile systems. Two 30mm Aden cannons could be fitted forward of the ventral fuel tank. For reconnaissance duties, the under-fuselage rocket pack could be replaced by a five Vinten camera pod. The modified F.3 prototype had first flown on 1 November 1966 and was used for flight development before delivery to Saudi Arabia, but was lost on 6 February 1972 after an explosion in the gun bay.

The programme was administered by Airwork Services and the first pair of F.53s, 53-681 and 53-682 left Warton on 1 July 1968 for delivery to Dhahran, where the Lightning Conversion Unit (LCU) was located and seconded contract pilots were training Saudi pilots. Initial training was on flight conversion from F-86 Sabres, as armament was not carried. At the start, serviceability was poor while provision of spares became established and at 09.00 hrs temperatures were challenging at over 100°F (38°C). Temperatures continued to increase during the day, with cockpit components melting if the canopies were not kept open. The introduction of the ventral gun pack was not straightforward, as there was regular jamming of the cannons, which was only avoided by keeping the guns very clean—a process not helped by the windblown sand.

Above: Lightning F.6 XR770 in Saudi markings promoting the export sale. This aircraft first flew on 16 December 1966 and was delivered to 74 Squadron on 26 September 1966. (*BAE Systems*)

Below: Lightning F.6 XR770 in Royal Saudi Air Force markings being demonstrated at the Farnborough Air Show in September 1966 before delivery to 74 Squadron. (*BAE Systems*)

Above: Lightning F.53 G-27-2 55-666 was built as XR722 for the RAF, but became the first F.53 for the RSAF and was delivered on 28 August 1969. It is fitted with underwing unguided rocket pods and shows the ventral Aden Cannon pack. It also shows the cranked wing leading edges on a test flight prior to delivery. This aircraft was first flown on 23 January 1965 and delivered to Saudi Arabia on 5 December 1969 for 2 Squadron. It was destroyed in a crash on 6 February 1972 while with 6 Squadron. (*BAE Systems*)

Below: Export Lightning F.53 G-AWON in the Farnborough static park on 17 September 1968, with a display of external loads. This aircraft was first flown on 11 June 1968 and delivered to Saudi Arabia as 53-686 on 17 April 1969, where it served with 2 Squadron. On retirement of the Saudi Lightnings, it was bought back by BAe as ZF592 and is preserved at the City of Norwich Aviation Museum. (*Philip Birtles*)

Above: Saudi Lightning F.53 53-687 at the Farnborough Air Show on 17 September 1968 was also registered as G-AWOO and G27-57. This aircraft was first flown on 5 July 1968 and delivered to Jeddah on 17 April 1969. It served with 2 Squadron. (*Philip Birtles*)

Below: Saudi Lightning F.53 53-685/G-27-55 at Warton with a range of the armament, including underwing weapons pylons. This aircraft was first flown on 29 May 1968, delivered to Saudi Arabia on 31 January 1969 and was operated by 2 Squadron. On retirement of the Lightnings in Saudi Arabia, this aircraft was bought back by BAe as ZF591, but its fate is unknown. (*BAE Systems*)

Above: An unidentified Lightning F.53 at Warton showing the alternative Skyflash and Red Top missile packs, ventral camera pack, bombs and underwing unguided rocket packs. (*BAE Systems*)

Left: A trio of Saudi Lightning T.55s in formation prior to delivery to Saudi Arabia, consisting of 55-713 C, 55-714 D and 55-711 A. T.55 55-713 was first flown on 16 November 1967 and all are airborne from Coltishall for syllabus and pilot training on 2 February 1968. 55-713 was delivered to Saudi Arabia on 27 August 1969. 55-713 was bought back by BAe as ZF598 and is preserved at the Midland Air Museum. (*BAE Systems*)

On 26 November 1969, around 1,000 South Yemen ground troops occupied a Saudi strategic border post at El Wadi'ah, bringing the Saudi Lightnings into action. The airfield at Kharmis was not ideal as it was located on a 6,500-foot plateau, where the thin air resulted in high landing speeds of 230mph, close to the aircraft tyre limits. The thinner air at the altitude also made the tail parachute less effective, putting increased loads on the brakes. Despite these limitations, a dozen Lightning F.53s deployed to Kharnis from Dhahran in the first half of December 1969. Armament was 1,000lb bombs, 2-inch rockets and 30mm cannons, all of which were successful against the military incursion, the only loss incurred when F.53 697 had to be abandoned in February 1970 after a fire was caused by a rifle bullet hole in the No.1 reheat system. The pilot was successfully recovered.

Training with the LCU continued at Dhahran included live firing and dropping inert 1,000lb bombs with experienced F-86 pilots by an ex-RAF senior Airwork contract pilot instructors. This was sometimes led by a fully armed F.53, but occasionally a T.55 with QFI in the right-hand seat. The two-seat aircraft lacked the ability to carry bombs or other air-to-ground weapons, and the 30mm cannon installation was often unreliable. With the completion of No.1 course, the runway at Dhahran needed resurfacing, moving four aircraft to Riyadh in May 1970 where temperatures could reach 180°F / 82°C. The only relief for the pilots was air-ventilated suits preset at maximum cold, but didn't function until the throttles were up to 80 per cent power, when the pilot went from extreme high temperature to near freezing in a fraction of a second. On arrival at Riyadh, the Lightnings were grounded for modifications to the fuel systems, resulting in no flying for the No.2 course. During 1971, the LCU achieved its full complement of trainers with three QFIs, three weapons instructors, an operational instructor and four simulator instructors, mostly seconded from the RAF.

Lightning F.53 53-699 P LCU on approach to Dhahran. This aircraft was first flown on 23 December 1968, delivered to Jeddah on 3 June 1969 and was operated by 6 Squadron. (*Adrian Balch collection*)

Lightning T.55 55-715 D LCU was first flown on 28 February 1968 and was delivered to Saudi Arabia on 11 March 1969. (*Adrian Balch collection*)

In 1973, BAC took responsibility for the Saudi contract and two CFS trained RSAF pilots were added to the British trainers.

A passing out parade was held by the LCU with King Faisal present on 3 December 1974, when in addition to formation aerobatics by five Lightnings, there was a formation fly over by sixteen. Unfortunately, the King was assassinated in the spring of 1975, but after a brief delay, conversion training was resumed alongside 2 Squadron, which had formed in 1969 at Dhahran with the LCU. Live air-to-air gunnery practice was provided by target towing 100 Squadron RAF Canberras and in 1976, 2 Squadron moved to King Faisal Air Base at Tabuk in the northwest of the country. In May 1977, the LCU disbanded on completion of Course No.13 having converted severnty-one pilots and was replaced by 13 Squadron with the RAF instructors returned to Britain, leaving four British contract pilots and a number of Saudi instructors. RSAF 6 Squadron had been operating Lightnings since 1966, but disbanded at Kharmis in 1977, with pilots and aircraft shared out among 2 Squadron at Tabuk and 13 Squadron at Dhahran.

With no new students for 13 Squadron in 1978, the instructors concentrated on weapons training and practice QRAs. Original 2-inch rocket practice at the LCU had only allowed two rockets to be fired, but as 13 Squadron was an operational unit, up to the total load of forty-two rockets could be carried in the retractable packs, with the three central tubes left empty to allow clearance for the doors to close, and the nosewheel to lock down.

No.15 was the final Lightning conversion course in 1981, with the first replacement RSAF F-15s arriving in December. For the first two months of 1982, 13 Squadron were operating both Lightnings and F-15s. At the end of February, all the remaining Lightnings joined 2 Squadron at Tabuk, and the last Lightnings were replaced with 2 Squadron in 1986 by F-5s.

Above: Lightning F.53 227 with 2 Squadron, armed with Firestreaks and unguided rocket pods. (*BAE Systems*)

Below: Lightning F.53s 1301 and 1302 with 2 Squadron armed with Red Tops over the featureless desert. (*Hedley Molland*)

Lightning F.53s 211 and 207 with 2 Squadron over the Tabuk Desert. (*Hedley Molland*)

All surviving 22 Lightnings were bought back by BAe as part of the contract for Tornados and they were flown back to Britain by RAF pilots from Binbrook. Saudi markings were replaced by RAF roundels and serial numbers ZF577 to ZF598. They were flown to Warton in two waves, twelve on 14 January 1986 and remaining ten on 22 January. BAe hoped to sell the aircraft to Austria and Nigeria, but neither placed an order, and the deteriorating aircraft were given to museums. Despite disappointing overseas sales, the Saudi Lightnings opened up opportunities for considerable exports of initially Tornadoes, then Typhoons in major weapons provision to Saudi Arabia in later years.

The only other Lightning export was when an order came from Kuwait in December 1966 for twelve F.53K fighters and a pair of T.55K operational trainers, in addition to twelve Strikemasters. In support of the aircraft, Britain would also supply flying and weapons instructors, as well as full support in engineering and spares.

After Kuwait gained independence from Britain in June 1961, a threat came from Iran, who planned to take over the country; under the terms of a defence treaty, military support was requested by Sheikh Abdullah Al-Salim Al-Sabah, the Kuwait leader. In response, Britain launched Operation Vantage, which included the deployment of a large naval task force together with a squadron of Hawker Hunters, successfully deterring any aggression. With the withdrawal of the British forces, the existing RAF base in nearby Bahrain was strengthened with a detachment of Hunter FGA.9s to provide protection for Kuwait, until they were withdrawn in 1971. The Kuwait Air Force (KAF) was also equipped with six Hunter FGA.56s and five T.57 trainers from 1965. The Lightnings were intended to provide a more modern and capable air defence capability, replacing the Hunters. KAF Lightning armament was similar to the Saudi Arabian aircraft, consisting of retractable rocket packs under the

Lightning F.53 G-AXEE 53-418 Kuwait Air Force at Le Bourget on 2 June 1969 armed with wing-mounted unguided RP, plus rocket pack under cockpit. This aircraft was first flown on 25 April 1969 and delivered to Jeddah on 11 July 1969. (*Philip Birtles*)

nose, underwing pylons for RP or 1,000lb bombs and 30mm Aden guns forward of the ventral fuel tank.

The first Lightning for Kuwait was T.55K 55-410 which was flown from Samlesbury on 24 May 1968, followed by F.53K 53-412; the majority of the Kuwait aircraft followed the Saudi Lightnings on the production line. These first two Lightnings departed Warton on 18 December 1968, flown by RAF pilots and followed the Saudi delivery route to the Middle East, arriving at Jeddah. The following day, a transit was made to Riyadh for refuelling and then the 50-minute flight to Kuwait International Airport. Further deliveries began in March 1969, with some flying by a more northerly route due to conflict between Israel and their Arab neighbours over the Red Sea. The RAF air and ground crews were usually on detachment in Kuwait for two months at a time and final deliveries were F.53s 53-422 and 53-423 on 4 December 1969.

Training of Kuwait Hunter pilots started in May 1968 with two T.55Ks and two F.53s, but was slow to start as the full support package had yet to be available due to unservicabilities and shortage of spares. This resulted in one Lightning being cannibalised for spare parts. By the middle of year, the serviceable Lightnings were used to keep pilots—who had gone solo—current, with later pilots attending ground school and maintaining flying skills with Hunters. Training was assisted by the arrival of a Lightning simulator. In addition to student training, the instructors needed to stay current on type, maintaining operational capability with low level practice interceptions assisted by a Royal Navy radar picket frigate. The second T.55K was delivered in December 1969, and with the spares situation improving, type conversion

Above: Mixed formation of Kuwait Lightning T.55 55-410 G27-78 A with XR759 and a Kuwait F.53 with underwing RP pods. This was the first of two T.55s for Kuwait and was first flown on 24 May 1968. It was delivered to Jeddah on 18 December 1968. (*BAE Systems*)

Below: Kuwait Lightning T.55 55-410 F27-78 in full national markings. (*BAE Systems*)

Kuwait Lightning F.53 53-423 R in Kuwait on 3 March 1971. This was the last of twelve F.53s for Kuwait and was first flown on 11 September 1969. It was delivered to Jeddah on 3 December 1969. (*Robbie Shaw*)

was restarted. Once more pilots were converted to type, weapons training was able to progress, with an additional weapons instructor arriving in September. With their Hunter experience, the pilots were already trained to a high standard and soon became accustomed to supersonic flying, although the main duties were ground attack in support of land troops. The daily flying training programme, in addition to conversion to type, also included high, medium and low-level attack profiles releasing bombs and firing rockets and cannons; the rocket pack replacing air-to-air missiles which were not required. The flight refuelling probes fitted for the delivery flights were RAF property and returned after arrival, as there were no flight refuelling tankers available within Kuwait.

Despite the improved rate of conversions and operations, five years after the first delivery, the KAF decided it needed an easier aircraft to support and in 1973 an abortive attempt was made to sell the aircraft to Egypt. A year later, Mirage F.1CKs and two-seat F.1BKs were ordered for the air defence role and A-4KU Skyhawks for ground attack, with deliveries starting in 1976. Following withdrawal from operations, the survivors were placed in external storage at Kuwait Airport, with some placed as gate guards at various KAF bases, used for technical training or donated to museums. Many were destroyed during Iraq's invasion of Kuwait in August 1990 and the later Gulf War. Of the three forming the 'Triplet' memorial at the F/A-18 base at Ahmed Al Jaber, at least one was blown off its plinth by a windstorm in 2018.

9
Thunder City

Barry Pover was one of a number of individuals who had the dream of putting a Lightning back in the air in Britain after retirement from the RAF. However, he probably had the best chance as he had considerable knowledge of the aircraft and had collected a massive stock of spares including the consumables, which were vital in keeping the aircraft in day-to-day operation. In December 1992, he bought Lightning F.6s XP693 and XR773, later adding T.5 XS451. Because BAC had flown Lightnings on the British civil register for demonstration purposes, he believed he could do the same and commenced a major overhaul of XP693 at Plymouth Airport. This was later moved to Exeter Airport, where the runway was more suitable for Lightning operations. However, the CAA did not support flying Lightnings as civil aircraft due to their complexity and the lack of British Aerospace and Rolls-Royce support with type design approval.

Then in January 1995, Mike 'Beachy' Head saw a Lightning for the first time when he visited Barry Pover's Classic Jets Company at Exeter Airport. Mike had bought two Hunters and a Canberra at a Sotheby's auction in November 1994 and was going to be trained to fly the Hunters in preparation for a ferry flight to his base at Cape Town in South Africa. Barry invited Mike to sit in the cockpit of XP693, which convinced Mike that he wanted to add one to his collection. The F.6s were complete, but not airworthy, but the availability of a two-seat aircraft was going to be essential. Still at Plymouth Executive Aviation was T.5 XS451 in poor condition, but Arnold Glass had bought six Lightnings which were abandoned at Cranfield, one of which was T.5 XS452, kept in taxiing condition by a group of volunteers led by Tony Hulls. Mike visited Cranfield in late 1995 with the SA CAA Chief Flying Inspector to inspect the aircraft. Despite the aircraft being kept outside during the typical winter weather, covered by tarpaulins held down by tyres, it was in overall good condition and was given a successful fast taxi run by Keith Hartley, a BAe test pilot. As a result, Mike bought the aircraft.

Preparations were then made to return the aircraft to airworthiness, and to assist in the delivery flight to Cape Town, Mike bought a couple of Buccaneers with one configured as a flight refuelling tanker to support the Lightning delivery flight. The other Buccaneer, XW988/ZU-AVI was flown to Cape Town in April 1966. The South African SAA inspectors arrived in Britain with Mike to certify XS452 and approve the aircraft for a test flight, with a test permit issued, before visiting the British CAA at Gatwick. Unfortunately, the British CAA made it quite clear that under no circumstances would they allow a Lightning to fly in British airspace, even on a South

African permit. The team returned to South Africa and Buccaneer XW987/ZU-BCR was flown out, as it was no longer required for the delivery flight.

The decision was made to ship XS452 to South Africa and in the late spring of 1997, three South African engineers arrived at Cranfield and with additional help from British engineers began to dismantle the aircraft, and as it had by now been removed from the hangar. Four 40-foot containers were ordered and a basic hangar erected to shelter the aircraft during dismantling. Every removal was carefully logged and all the wires identified to avoid problems on reassembly. During this process, a number of minor faults were identified and corrected before shipping. This work took nearly three months to complete, ready for shipping to South Africa, and by the autumn of 1997 it was ready to go.

With XS452 on its way, Mike bought the two F.6s and the T.5 XS451 from Mach 2 Enterprises, of which Barry Pover was one of a three-man partnership. The deal included a massive amount of spares, and another engineering team arriving soon after the departure of the first T.5. The three aircraft and spares required forty-eight 40-foot containers, which arrived at Cape Town International Airport in the spring of 1997 over a period of three weeks. To house the major rebuild and restoration programme, a new 2,800 square metre facility was constructed at the Airport, which was called the Aircraft Maintenance and Refurbishment Centre (AMARC). One of the major challenges was the correct reassembly of the wings as no jigs existed and XS452 was the first aircraft to be assembled using some of the spares, which had to be located in the vast collection. In February 1998, it was wheeled out in an overall gloss black

Lightning T.5 XS452/ZU-BBD in overall gloss black carrying the markings of 11 Squadron. This aircraft was first flown on 30 June 1965 and delivered to 226 OCU on 20 September 1965. It is expected to be preserved at Binbrook as part of the growing Lightning collection. (*Ian Black*)

paint scheme, following the concept of the ex-Black Arrows Hunter F.6 acquired at the auction, when the engines were run.

By this time, Mike had formed Thunder City Holdings (Pty) Ltd to operate a fleet of classic British jets. In addition to the four Lightnings, the fleet also included three Buccaneers and seven Hunters. As well as being available to perform at air shows, they could also be chartered for passenger experience flights, test pilot training and development of new advanced systems. The South African CAA agreed that the first flight should be from the Test Flight and Development Centre (TFDC) on the coast at the southern tip of Africa to avoid flying initially over a built-up area. Following a satisfactory flight test programme, the aircraft could return to Cape Town. Permission to fly the Lightning from TFDC was obtained and after clearing any snags from the engine ground runs with Keith Hartley in the left-hand seat and Mike in the right, XW452 made its first post restoration flight on 18 March 1998. With the completion of the flight test programme, the SA CAA issued the Certificate of Airworthiness (C of A) allowing the training of Mike to commence, achieving clearance to go solo and flying over 100 sorties.

Meanwhile, work had started with the demanding rebuild of T.5 XS451. The aircraft was incomplete, but had very low fatigue index and the basic airframe was in very good condition. Using some 90 per cent of new parts in the comprehensive stock of spares, the aircraft was rebuilt, including fitting a VHF radio in place of the RAF UHF system. The cockpit was rebuilt and rewired to as-new condition, the entire project using the experience from XS452. From the start to engine runs took fourteen months, as the aircraft was in such good condition and as it had never previously been painted, it retained its natural metal finish. It was taken for its first test flight again by Keith Hartley and on completion was awarded its C of A.

Lightning T.5 XS451/ZU-BEX in the markings of the LTU. This aircraft crashed fatally on 14 November 2009, ending flight operations of Thunder City. It was first flown on 3 June 1965 and delivered to 5 Squadron on 19 November 1965. It received Cat 3 damage at Binbrook in December 1969 and was allocated maintenance serial 8503M. (*Ian Black*)

With XS451 flying, F.6 XR773 was ready for assembly with both engine bays stripped and completely rebuilt with new engines and reheat pipes fitted. It was ready for its first flight, after around 13 years since the type had been withdrawn by the RAF, on 4 November 2001 with Mike in command. Following award of the C of A certificate, XR773 made her display debut on 15 December 2001 at the Stellenbosch Airshow. At this stage, F.6 XP693 was being surveyed in preparation for its rebuild, which was successfully completed. This aircraft had been rebuilt to a very high standard by Barry Pover's team at Exeter before being bought by Mike. This Lightning had never seen RAF service, having been part of the BAe test fleet at Warton and was never painted.

All flying later ceased when T.5 XS451 crashed on 14 November 2009 during an air display, killing the pilot Dave Stock. The cause of the accident was hydraulic failure after a fire in the rear fuselage. It was found in the subsequent investigation that the seat and canopy mechanisms had failed and had not been serviced, resulting in Thunder City's Air Operating Certificate being withdrawn in March 2010. There were found to be major shortcomings in the company's maintenance programme. On 9 September 2010, Thunder City stopped passenger flights and the final airshow appearance was on 27 April 2012, with the aircraft having been put up for sale on 22 August 2011. Sadly, Mike died of a sudden heart attack on 21 May 2017 at the age of 59. In late 2021, Hangar 51 Aviation, owned by Jay Smith, acquired part of the collection with plans to return some to flight, but XP693 was not included and in 2023 it was bought by Ian Black, to join his other Lightning preserved at Binbrook.

Lightning F.6 XR773/ZU-BEW in 11 Squadron markings. This aircraft was first flown on 28 February 1966 and was delivered to 74 Squadron on 7 November 1966. It was then passed to 56 Squadron in Cyprus. It is believed to be stored at Cape Town. (*Ian Black*)

Lightning F.6 XP693/ZU-BEY never served with the RAF and was used for manufacturers and service development programmes. This aircraft is owned by Ian Black and is stored at Binbrook, where it arrived on 10 July 2023. (*Ian Black*)

The Thunder City Lightning fleet lined up at Cape Town. (*Ian Black*)

Appendix 1

Lightning Production

Mark	Number	Identities	Remarks
P1A prototypes	3	WG760, WG763, WG765	WG765 structural test and not flown
P1B prototypes	3	XA847, XA853, XA856	XA856 to R-R for Avon development.
P1B pre-production	20	XG307–XG337	
T.4 prototypes	2	XL628, XL629	XL628 crashed 1.10.59
F.1	20	XM134–XM168	XM168 structural test and not flown
F.1A	24	XM169–XM218	XM217 & XM218 not built
T.4	20	XM966–XM997	
F.2	44	XN723–XN735 XN767–XN797	
F.3	70	XP693–XP708 XP735–XP765 XR711–XR728 XR747–XR751	
F.3/6	16	XR752–XR767	Interim F.6s
F.6	39	XR768–XR773 XS893–XS903 XS918–XS938	
T.5	22	XS416–XS423 XS449–XS460 XV328–XV329	
T.55 Saudi	6	55-711–55-716	
T.55 Kuwait	2	55-410–55-411	
F.53 Saudi	33	53-667–53-699	
F.53 Saudi	1	53-700	Last production Lightning, replaced 53-690 which crashed before delivery
F.53 Kuwait	12	53-412–53-423	

Appendix 2

RAF Lightning Squadrons

Unit	Base	Mark	Dates
5 Squadron	Binbrook	F.6	12.65–db 31.12.87
		F.1A	6.70–9.72
		F.3	10.72–9.87
11 Squadron	rf Leuchars	F.6	4.67–db 30.4.88
	Binbrook		28.3.72
		F.3	10.72–5.86
19 Squadron	Leconfield	F.2	17.12.62–10.69
	Gutersloh		23.9.65
		F.2A	1.68–db 31.12.76
23 Squadron	Leuchars	F.3	8.64–11.67
		F.6	5.67–10.75
		F.3	5.72–db 31.10.75
29 Squadron	Wattisham	F.3	10.5.67–db 31.12.74
56 Squadron	Wattisham	F.1A	14.12.60–4.65
		F.3	3.65–12.76
	Akrotiri, Cyprus		11.4.67
		F.6	9.71
	Wattisham		21.1.75–db 28.6.75
74 Squadron	Coltishall	F.1	6.60–4.64
	Leuchars		2.3.64
		F.3	4.64–9.67
		F.6	9.66–8.71
	Tengah, Singapore		12.6.67–db 1.9.71
92 Squadron	Leconfield	F.2	23.1.63–7.71
	Geilenkirchen		29.12.65
	Gutersloh		24.1.68
		F.2A	8.68 db 31.3.77

Unit	Base	Mark	Dates
111 Squadron	Wattisham	F.1A	13.4.61–2.65
		F.3	12.64
		F.6	5.74 db 30.9.74
226 OCU	Middleton St George	F.1, T.4	7.63
	Coltishall	F.3, T.5	4.64–30.9.74

Appendix 3

Specifications

Mark	Power	Weights	Dimensions	Performance	Stores
P1A	2×Armstrong Siddeley Sapphires			Mach 1.5+	None
P1A No.2	2×Armstrong Siddeley Sapphires			Mach 1.5+	2×30mm cannons
P1B/ F.1	2×R-R Avon 24R 14,430lb thrust	25,753lb	Span 34ft 10in Length 50ft Height 17ft 6in	Mach 2.3/1,280mph Ceiling 55,000ft	2×30mm cannons + 2×Firestreaks
F.1A	2×R-R Avon 24R 14,430lb thrust	25,737lb	Span 34ft 10in Length 55ft 3in Height 19ft 7in	Mach 2.3/1,280mph	2×30mm cannons + 2×Firestreaks
F.2	2×R-R Avon 24R 14,430lb thrust		Span 34ft 10in Length 55ft 3in Height 19ft 7in	Mach 2.3/1,280mph Ceiling 60.000ft	2×30mm cannons + 2×Firestreaks
F.3	2×R-R Avon 300 16,300lb thrust	26,905lb	Span 34ft 10in Length 55ft 3in Height 19ft 7in	Mach 2.3/1,280mph Ceiling 60,000ft	2×Firestreaks or 2 Red Tops
T.4	2×R_R Avon 24R 14,430lb thrust		Span 34ft 10in Length 55ft 3in Height 19ft 7in	Mach 2.3/1,280mph Ceiling 55,000ft	2×Firestreaks
T.5	R-R Avon 300 16,360lb thrust	Max take-off 40,140lb	Span 34ft 10in Length 55ft 3in Height 19ft 7in	Mach 2.2 Ceiling 60,000ft	2×Firestreaks or 2×Red Tops
F.6	R-R Avon 302 16,300lb thrust	Empty 28,041lb Max take-off 41,700lb	Span 34ft 10in Length 55ft 3in Height 19ft 7in	Mach 2.3/1,280mph Ceiling 60,000ft	2×Red Tops 2×30mm cannons 2×260-gallon overwing fuel tanks.

Mark	Power	Weights	Dimensions	Performance	Stores
F.53	R-R Avon 302 16,300lb thrust	Empty 28,041lb Max take-off 41,700lb	Span 34ft 10in Length 55ft 3in Height 19ft 7in	Mach 2.3/1,280mph Ceiling 60,000ft	2×Red Top 2×30mm cannons + 144 2 in RP, 6×1,000lb bombs, 2×MATRA 155 18 SNEB 68mm RP
T.55	R-R Avon 3402 16,300lb thrust	Max take-off 40,140lb	Span 34ft 10in Length 55ft 3in Height 19ft 7in	Mach 2.3/1,280mph Ceiling 60,000ft	2×Red Tops

Appendix 4

Preserved Lightnings

If there is a star in the 'Markings' column, see below for a photograph of the aircraft.

Identity	Mark	Location	Markings
WG760	P.1A	RAF Museum, Cosford	Prototype *
WG763	P.1A	Boscombe Down Aviation Collection, Old Sarum	Prototype *
XA847	P.1B	Stored Kettleburgh, Suffolk	Prototype *
XG329	F.1	Norfolk & Suffolk Aviation Museum, Flixton, Norfolk	
XG337	F.1	RAF Museum, Cosford	
XM135	F.1	IWM Duxford, Cambridgeshire	74 Squadron *
XM172	F.1A	Lakes Lightnings, Spark Bridge, Cumbria	226 OCU *
XM173	F.1A	Dyson Ltd, Malmesbury, Wiltshire	
XM178	F.1A	Association des Amis du Musee du Chateau, Savigny-les-Beaune, France	
XM192	F.1A	Thorpe Camp, Woodhall Spa, Lincolnshire	111 Squadron *
XN730	F.2A	Gatow, Berlin, Germany	
XN776	F.2A	National Museum of Flight, East Fortune, Scotland	
XN782	F.2A	Luftfahtausstellung Museum, Hermeskeil	
XN784	F.2A	Zruc Air Park, Pilsen, Czech Republic.	
XP706	F.3	S Yorks Aircraft Museum, Doncaster	
XP745	F.3	Vanguard Haulage, Greenford Greater London	
XR713 (XR718)	F.3	Lightning Preservation Group, Bruntingthorpe	111 Squadron *
XR718	F.3	Over Dinsdale, Darlington, Durham	
XR749	F.3	Glenugie Engineering, Peterhead, Aberdeen	LTF *
XL629	T.4	Boscombe Down	ETPS
XS416	T.5	Binbrook, Lincolnshire	
XS417	T.5	Newark Air Museum, Winthorpe, Nottinghamshire	LTF *

Identity	Mark	Location	Markings
XS420	T.5	FAST Farnborough, Hampshire	226OCU/145 Squadron *
XS422	T.5	Anglo-American Lightning Organisation, Stennis International Airport, USA (restoration to fly)	
XS456	T.5	Skegness Airfield, Lincolnshire	
XS458	T.5	Cranfield, Bedfordshire	92 Squadron *
XS459	T.5	Binbrook, Lincolnshire	5 Squadron *
XS452	T.5	Cape Town, South Africa, stored & for sale	ZU-BBD
XP693	F.6	Binbrook, Lincolnshire	
XR724	F.6	Binbrook, Lincolnshire	5 Squadron *
XR725	F.6	Chestnut Farm Binbrook, Lincolnshire	
XR728	F.6	Lightning Preservation Group, Bruntingthorpe, Leicestershire	LTF *
XR753	F.6	RAF Coningsby, Lincolnshire	11 Squadron
XR755	F.6	Callington, Cornwall	
XR770	F.6	RAF Manston History Museum, Kent	
XR771	F.6	Midland Air Museum, Coventry, Warwickshire	11 Squadron *
XR773	F.6	Cape Town International Airport, stored	ZU-BEW
XS897	F.6	RAF Coningsby, Lincolnshire	XP765 29 Squadron *
XS903	F.6	Yorkshire Air Museum, Elvington	11 Squadron *
XS904	F.6	Lightning Preservation Group, Bruntingthorpe, Leicestershire	11 Squadron *
XS919	F.6	Henstridge Airfield, Somerset, - stored	
XS925	F.6	RAF Museum, Hendon, London	11 Squadron *
XS928	F.6	BAE Systems, Warton, Lancashire	
XS929	F.6	RAF Akrotiri, Cyprus	56 Squadron
XS936	F.6	Castle Motors, Liskeard, Cornwall	111 Squadron *
52-610	F.52	Saqr al Jazira Museum, Royadh, Saudi Arabia	Ex-XN770
53-412	F.53	Kuwait International Airport, Kuwait	
53-418	F.53	Educational Science Museum, Kuwait	
53-420	F.53	Kuwait Technology Institute	
53-421	F.53	MOD Mubarak Camp HQ, Kuwait City	
53.422	F.53	RKAFB Ali Al Salem, Kuwait	
53-423	F.53	RKAFB Ali Al Salem, Kuwait	
53-671	F.53	Gatwick Aviation Museum, Charlwood, Surrey	
ZF578 53-670	F.53	Tangmere Military Aviation Museum, West Sussex	XR753 23 Squadron *

Identity	Mark	Location	Markings
ZF580 53-672	F.53	Cornwall Aviation Heritage Centre, RAF St Mawgan, since closed	XS935 5 Squadron. For sale?
ZF581 53-675	F.53	Bentwaters Cold War Museum, Suffolk	Restoration to running condition *
ZF583 53-681	F.53	Solway Aviation Museum, Carlisle Airport, Cumbria	*
ZF584 53-682	F.53	Dumfries & Galloway Aviation Museum, Scotland	
ZF588 53-693	F.53	East Midlands Aeropark, Castle Donnington, Derbyshire	74 Squadron *
ZF592 53-686	F.53	City of Norwich Aviation Museum, Horsham St Faith, Norfolk	RSAF 53-686
ZF593 53-692	F.53	Pima Air & Space Museum, Tucson, Arizona, USA	29 Squadron *
ZF594 53-696	F.53	NE Land, Sea & Air Museum, Sunderland	11 Squadron *
XM992 54-651	T.54	Prince Sultan Air Base, Saudi Arabia	54-608
ZF598 55-713	T.55	Midland Air Museum, Coventry Airport, Warwickshire	RSAF *
55-716	T.55	Saqr al Jazira Museum, Riyadh, Saudi Arabia	

First prototype P.1A WG760/7755M preserved at the RAF Museum, Cosford since January 1986 and noted in October 1993. This aircraft was first flown by R. Beamont on 4 August 1954 (*Philip Birtles*)

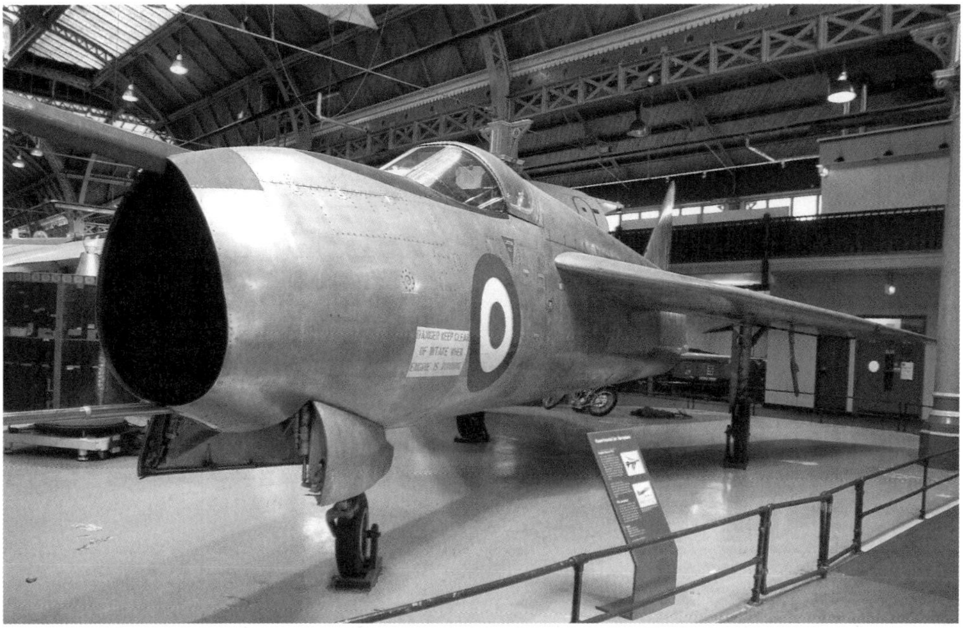

Above: Second prototype P.1A WG763/7816M when it was preserved in Manchester, but was moved on 2 February 2022 to the Boscombe Down Aviation Collection at Old Sarum. This aircraft was first flown on 18 July 1955 and was introduced to the public for the first time at the Farnborough Show in September 1955. On retirement, it went to RAF Henlow for ground instruction. (*Philip Birtles*)

Below: First of three P.1B prototypes, XA847 static at Farnborough in September 1994 fitted with a dorsal fillet. This aircraft was first flown on 4 April 1957 and reached Mach 1.2 during that flight. It was also the first British aircraft to reach Mach 2 on 25 November 1958. It was put on display in the RAF Museum at Hendon in mid-1972, but replaced by F.6 XS925 in April 1988, as a more representative RAF aircraft. It is stored, dismantled and under cover at Kettleburgh, Suffolk. (*Philip Birtles*)

Above: Lightning F.1 XM135 B 74 Squadron at IWM Duxford noted 11 August 2014. This aircraft was first flown on 14 November 1959 and delivered to the CFE, Coltishall on 25 May 1960. It went to 226 OCU in September 1963, followed by the Leuchars TFF. It was stored at 60 MU from 28 June 1971 and flew to the IWM on 20 November 1974, having flown 1,343 hours. (*Philip Birtles*)

Below: Lightning F.1A XM172/8427M 226 OCU gate guard at Coltishall, noted on 18 November 1980. This aircraft was first flown on 10 October 1960 and was the first F.1A to enter service when it was delivered to 56 Squadron on 14 December 1960. It joined 226 OCU on 4 May 1963 and was withdrawn from use on 10 July 1974. (*Philip Birtles*)

Above: Lightning F.1A XM172 was stored at Booker from 1999 until April 2002, with a static appearance at Farnborough in July 2000, before going to Lakes Lightnings at Spark Bridge in Cumbria where it is on display in a private garden. (*Philip Birtles*)

Below: Lightning F.1A XM192 K 111 Squadron at Tattershall Thorpe Camp on 21 June 2016. This aircraft was first flown on 25 May 1961 and delivered to 111 Squadron on 28 June 1961. It was issued to 226 OCU on 14 January 1965 and then Binbrook and Wattisham TFF. It was retired on 4 January 1974 when it became 8413M, taking up guard duties at Wattisham gate on 28 May 1974 until it was sold in 1994. (*Philip Birtles*)

Above: Lightning F.3 XR713 111 Squadron at Bruntingthorpe on 5 June 2017. This aircraft was first flown on 21 October 1964 and delivered to 111 Squadron on 8 January 1965. It was later with 5 Squadron and LTF until being grounded as 8935M as gate guardian at Leuchars on 9 March 1987. With the closure of RAF Leuchars, it was moved to Bruntingthorpe in May 2015 and is seen being painted ready for unveiling on 23 July 2017. Unlike the Lightning F.6s on site, this aircraft is not functional. (*Philip Birtles*)

Below: Lightning F.3 XR749 DA LTF on the gate at Middleton St George on 12 July 2000. This aircraft was first flown on 30 April 1965 and was delivered to 56 Squadron on 4 October 1967. It joined 5 Squadron on 30 October 1972 and 11 then Squadron on 10 December 1982. It was withdrawn from use on 9 February as 8926M, and later to Leuchars as 8934M for BDR before being sold privately and put on the gate to Teeside Airport. It is now preserved with Glenugie Engineering at Peterhead, Aberdeen. (*Philip Birtles*)

Above: Lightning T.5 XS417 DZ LTF at Newark Air Museum, noted 21 June 2017. This aircraft was the first T.5 to fly on 17 July 1964 and delivered to 226 OCU on 25 May 1965 after being used for some development flying. It served with 23 Squadron from 21 December 1967, 56 Squadron from 20 October 1975, 11 Squadron from 14 December 1979 and 5 Squadron from 4 February 1983 before joining the LTF. It last flew on 18 May 1987 and was moved by road to Newark Air Museum on 29 July 1988. (*Philip Birtles*)

Below: Lightning T.5 XS420 226 OCU on static display at Fairford on 18 July 2003. This aircraft was first flown on 23 January 1965 and was delivered to 226 OCU on 29 April 1965. It served with LTF from 20 September 1976. It was last flown in May 1983 and withdrawn from use on 1 June 1983 for spares and Binbrook decoy. It was moved by road to Wellesley Aviation at Narborough on 25 July 1988 and acquired by FAST at Farnborough on 3 September 2003, where it is normally displayed. (*Philip Birtles*)

Above: Lightning T.5 XS458 92 Squadron at Cranfield on 17 September 2016. This aircraft was first flown on 3 December 1965 and was delivered to 226 OCU on 2 February 1966. It was issued to 5 Squadron on 30 September 1975, followed by 11 Squadron on 29 August 1982, then LTF on 7 August 1986. It was withdrawn from use on 21 April 1987 and bought by Arnold Glass, who had it flown into Cranfield on 29 June 1988. It became derelict until rescued by Russell Carpenter and team, who restored it to working condition and display it with examples of all the Lightning squadron identities. (*Philip Birtles*)

Opposite above: Lightning T.5 XS459 AW 5 Squadron at Wisbech on 22 June 1996. This aircraft was first flown on 18 December 1965 and was delivered to 226 OCU, later going to 29, 56 Squadrons, LTF and 5 Squadron. It was struck off charge on 21 June 1988. It was part of the collection at a garden centre near Wisbech, and when the aircraft collection was disposed of, it went to Binbrook by May 2021. (*Philip Birtles*)

Opposite below: Lightning F.6 XR724/G-BTSY AE 5 Squadron stored at Binbrook on 27 July 2011. This aircraft was first flown on 10 February 1965 and built as an F.3, but converted to F.6 before delivery to 11 Squadron on 16 June 1967. It went to 5 Squadron on 14 April 1986 and then to Warton on 12 April 1988 for Tornado F.3 radar trials. It was withdrawn from use on 27 June 1990 and stored at Shawbury, from where it was sold to the Lightning Association and flown to Binbrook on 23 July 1992. After a period of neglect, this aircraft is being brought back to working order. (*Philip Birtles*)

AW
XS459

AE

Above: Lightning F.6 XR728 JS LTF at Bruntingthorpe on a damp 5 June 2017. This aircraft was first flown on 17 April 1965 as an F.3, but converted to F.6 before delivery to 23 Squadron at Leuchars on 30 October 1967. It went to 56 Squadron at Akrotiri on 15 December 1973, which moved to Wattisham on 31 January 1975. It joined 5 Squadron on 27 June 1978 and then LTF, making its last service flight on 23 May 1988 after a total of 3,708 hours 40 minutes. It was bought by the Lightning Preservation Group and delivered by air on 24 June 1988 to Bruntingthorpe, where it is kept in working order. (*Philip Birtles*)

Below: Lightning F.6 XR771 BF 11 Squadron at Midland Air Museum Coventry on 11 May 2010. This aircraft was first flown on 20 January 1966 and delivered to 74 Squadron on 24 October 1956, before flying to Singapore in June 1967. It was delivered to 56 Squadron in Cyprus in September 1971 and flown back with the squadron to Wattisham on 31 January 1975. It went to 5 Squadron on 30 October 1980, then 11 Squadron on 2 March 1983, returning to 11 Squadron on 4 January 1988. Its last flight was on 15 March 1988, when it had achieved 3,554 flying hours. It was withdrawn from use on 21 March 1988 and sold to the Midland Air Museum, where it arrived by road on 15 July 1988. (*Philip Birtles*)

Above: Lightning F.6 XS897 at Coningsby on 28 October 2016 outside the 29 Squadron hangar marked as XP765 A. This aircraft was first flown on 10 May 1966, was delivered to 74 Squadron at Leuchars on 21 December 1966 and went to Singapore in June 1967. With the disbandment of 74 Squadron, this aircraft was ferried back to 56 Squadron at Akrotiri on 7 September 1971. It went to 11 Squadron on 23 September 1977 and 5 Squadron on 7 April 1986 and made its last flight on 14 December 1987. It was sold in Doncaster in June 1988, and then to the South Yorkshire Air Museum at Firbeck in 1993. It was later acquired by 29 Squadron, who never operated Lightning F.6s. (*Philip Birtles*)

Below: Lightning F.6 XS903 BA 11 Squadron at Yorkshire Air Museum on 8 July 2014. This aircraft was first flown on 17 August 1966 and delivered to 5 Squadron on 17 March 1967. It moved to 11 Squadron on 14 October 1980. It was withdrawn from use on 4 May 1988 and delivered to the Yorkshire Air Museum on 18 May 1988. (*Philip Birtles*)

Above: Lightning F.6 XS904 BQ 11 Squadron in a HAS at Bruntingthorpe on 5 June 2017. This aircraft was first flown on 22 September 1966 and delivered to 11 Squadron on 19 April 1967. It was flown into Bruntingthorpe on 21 January 1993 for the Lightning Preservation Group, which keeps the aircraft in working order. (*Philip Birtles*)

Below: Lightning F.6 XS925 BA 11 Squadron in the RAF Museum at Hendon on 28 March 1993, where it was delivered on 26 April 1988. (*Philip Birtles*)

Above: Lightning F.6 XS936 dramatically mounted in spurious 111 Squadron markings at Castleair in Cornwall on 17 March 1991. It was delivered to the site on 23 June 1988 and mounted by the following year. (*Philip Birtles*)

Below: Lightning F.53 ZF578/53-670 at the Tangmere Military Aviation Museum on 31 July 2003, marked as F.6 XR758 A 23 Squadron. It arrived at the museum in June 2002. (*Philip Birtles*)

Above: Lightning F.53 ZF581/53-675 at the Bentwaters Cold War Museum on 15 May 1922 in a HAS being prepared for in depth restoration. It was delivered to the museum on 22 May 2011. (*Philip Birtles*)

Below: Lightning F.53 ZF583/53-681 at the Solway Aviation Museum on 4 July 1993. The aircraft was delivered by road from Warton on 8 January 1989 and is now in 56 Squadron markings. (*Philip Birtles*)

Above: Lightning F.53 ZF588/53-693 at East Midlands Aeropark on 23 March 1994, in the markings of L 74 Squadron fitted with overwing fuel tanks. It was delivered to the museum on 8 January 1989. (*Philip Birtles*)

Below: Lightning F.53 ZF593/53-692 at Warner Robbins AFB on 11 April 2001 in spurious 29 Squadron markings and has now been moved to the Pima Air & Space Museum in Arizona. (*Philip Birtles*)

Above: Lightning F.53 ZF594/53-696 at the North East Land, Sea and Air Museum marked as XE933 11 Squadron on 29 April 2019, where it was delivered in April 1989. (*Philip Birtles*)

Below: Lightning T.55 55-713/ZF598 at the Midland Air Museum on 11 May 2010 in full Saudi markings, where it was delivered on 14 January 1989. (*Philip Birtles*)